When Families End & Blend

Sophia Rantzau

Clink Street

London | New York

Published by Clink Street Publishing 2020

Copyright © 2020

First edition.

ISBN:
978-1-913568-25-2 - paperback
978-1-913568-26-9 - ebook

"Success is not final,
failure is not fatal,
It is the courage to continue that counts."

Winston Churchill

Contents

Foreword 11
Acknowledgements 13
Introduction 15
Welcome to Holland 21

1. You Are Not Alone 23
    1.1. Do what's right for YOU! 24
    1.2. Hindsight is a wonderful thing! 28

2. Separating 33
    2.1. HELP! We are splitting up 34
    2.2. Help! We're splitting up – AGAIN 39

3. Living arrangements 43
    3.1. Maintain or make a relationship with
          your child 44
    3.2. Your child and their homes 48
    3.3. The diversity of 'changeover week' 53
    3.4. Building a relationship with your stepchild ... 54

4. House Rules 61
    4.1. Sweet shop vs. grocery store 62

5. The Old Family, Now Revised 67
    5.1. What changes now mum/dad have gone? ... 68

6. **Feelings** **75**
   6.1. But this is how I feel!! – Couldn't you have tried harder to make it work? 76
   6.2. You think it's tough?! 80
   6.3. The estranged parent 84
   6.4. Piggy in the middle 88

7. **Take Responsibility** **93**
   7.1. Own it! 94
   7.2. Use your filter 98
   7.3. A child becomes a role figure/adult 102
   7.4. GPS – Guilty Parent Syndrome 106

8. **Different Ways To Have A Conversation** **111**
   8.1. Walking, driving, texting, communication book 112
   8.2. Listen and communicate: what did you just hear? 116

9. **The Ex!** **121**
   9.1. Stop slating your Ex to your child 122

10. **The New Relationship** **127**
   10.1. Your child is playing catch-up 129
   10.2. Don't force it – how would you like it? 133
   10.3. Making time for yourselves and your new partner 137
   10.4. Sleepovers help! 141

11. **A New Family** **145**
   11.1. How many 'parents' grandparents etc.? ... 146
   11.2. You're not my mum! 150

12. **You're getting married** **153**
   12.1. What's in a name? 154

13. **Celebration days** **159**
    13.1. Oh dear it's Christmas 160
    13.2. Mother's/Father's Day 164

14. **As Time Goes By** **169**
    14.1. Sometimes I'm sad – weeks/months later it can
          still be hard. 170
    14.2. The aftermath: what ghosts of Christmas past
          are you still carrying? 173

15. **Never underestimate a 'bully' word** **179**
    15.1. The shoulds and the oughts 180

16. **Counselling For Parents** **185**
    16.1. How about you the parent having counselling?
          Now there's a thought 186

References **191**

Foreword

I am a qualified counsellor and I run my private practice in Storrington, West Sussex.

I have been counselling clients since 2012 and during this time, many of my clients past and present have been affected through their families ending and blending, and indeed re-blending.

I have been a teenager within a nuclear family that divorced and have experienced my parents' partners come in and out of my life. I am a stepparent and in a previous relationship was a stepparent also.

I wished I had the knowledge then that I have now. I would go as far to say, that I would have liked this book at a time of me entering into a 'ready-made family', to help me understand the complications and indeed whether this is something that I wanted to consider embarking on. I also feel it may have helped reassure me that I wasn't on my own or thinking what I was experiencing was unique to me. In my personal and professional lives, I have and do on a daily basis encounter many blended families.

This book may provide you with an overview of some things that might happen and some of the areas I cover may not happen either. Look at this as a handbook – a ready reference aid – just like a first aid kit, this could be your go-to in times of 'separation and blended family emergencies'.

This book does not make me a 'know-it-all', however when I wrote a blog about blended families, it was the second most talked about blog which I have written. This got me thinking, what is out there for separating, separated, divorced, blended and re-blended families? – And so the book idea was born.

***

I often wonder what may have happened if I'd had counselling when my parents' separation and divorce kicked off. I had no idea (and why should I, I was 15 years old at the time) how the impact of my parents' separation would fester in my subconscious to then be played out in a variety of ways in my life.

I decided to get 'my version' of the divorce untangled once and for all. You could look at it a bit like a spring clean of your attic. There are scary and dark corners that you may not want to look at. There could also be boxes that you are curious to open. Once 'cleaned' and reorganised, your attic becomes exactly that, a place to store things that are of a positive use to you – result!

***

I'd like to think I was a 'regular' 15-year-old, and although aware that my parents had their ups and downs, it never seemed too serious to worry about. I remember one time when we were driving to our town to go shopping I was with my parents and sister. I was sitting in the back of the car probably being a 'moody' teenager and Phil Collins' 'Doesn't Anybody Stay Together Anymore?' was playing on the radio. I felt sad about that song, however I didn't realise at the time how close my parents had come to separating.

My mum's hurt extended to her sharing her pain with my sister and me. I was 15 and I didn't want this. I didn't want my parents to split up, and I definitely didn't want to be involved with any adult conversations.

I had literally (like minutes, or even hours before) just been asked out by a boy, whom I had had a serious crush on at the time. My heart was doing somersaults, the smile on my face was ridiculously large, I felt goofy, and it felt good. As I stepped out of my best friend's house (having just said goodbye to said brand spanking new boyfriend) to my mum who was frantically beeping the horn, something she never did and then in that split second, my life changed – FOREVER!

Acknowledgements

I would like to thank my clients for finding the courage to have counselling and allow to join them in their very private and personal journey. You all enable me to be the counsellor that I am today.

I would also like to share my love and gratitude to my husband, who had the courage to challenge me and for which I will be eternally grateful.

Introduction

This book does not have to be read cover to cover. If you have the time, I would recommend reading it all, as this could be seen as an investment for you and your child whether they are your own or stepchildren.

The aim of this book is to contribute in a positive way whether you are about to or are in the process of separating and also to help understand the dynamics of a new blended family.

Particularly if you are beginning a new relationship with children already 'in-situ', or considering what a blended family might be like and what differences there could be.

This book is not to dissuade you or put you off, this is purely a helpful handbook to get you through some potential pitfalls that comes with separation and a blended family. I do also share some 'highs' too – so I promise you, it's not all 'doom and gloom', just showing the trickier sides of separation and blended families. I could write a book about all the good times that I have encountered so far, but I am not sure that would get much interest!

But (and my English teacher Mrs Todd will be saying 'You can't start a sentence with BUT!' – sorry I just did), if you want to, you can just dip in and out of the chapters that may be relevant to you right now, or as and when issues come up.

Basically you will be pleased to hear that there is no right or wrong way of reading it. I am just really thrilled that you are doing so. If nothing else, hopefully this book will show you that a) you are not alone b) some of your worries and concerns may be explored in this book and c) you really are NOT alone!

***

I do mention that counselling could be an option at certain points in this book. Although I am a counsellor and totally see the positive effect of good counselling, I would also like you to see this as an option, as a possibility that you do not have to have all the answers and actually talking to a 'professional stranger' could indeed be really helpful to either you or your child.

I am not saying at every tricky situation you or your child 'should' have counselling but to hold this in mind.

***

When you read this book please note that as I refer to 'the child', there could of course in your case be several children in the family both biological and step. When I am giving a specific example of several children involved, this can of course be a single child situation.

I will also refer to the 'other' adult as a parent in certain examples for simplicity.

The above points are purely for grammatical ease, when you read through the book.

***

Blended families – those two words conjure up all sorts of pictures to me (I am a visual person and no doubt this will come out many times throughout this book.) Anyhow I digress!

When I visualise 'blended families', I see a row of smoothies, some bright green like the Incredible Hulk, it may look scary but like the Hulk, it could actually be a strong combination! The Incredible Hulk, was strong, determined and kind. A pink milkshake looks nice on the outside, but what's really going on in the inside?

I can imagine a picture of a blender with the entire contents sprayed across the kitchen along with covering the person operating the blender – yep I have definitely been part of that blended family, when I've looked around and said (hopefully not out loud) – what on earth happened here?! – or words to that effect!! Maybe I was convinced that I had kept a 'lid' on my feelings and maybe at that moment I hadn't!

The point for me is that you can make a smoothie with the same ingredients day in day out, but it doesn't always taste the same or pan out how you thought it would. That to me is no different to blended families. The raspberries that normally taste so sweet are a bit tart today and a family member, usually so sweet, may also be a bit unpleasant too at times. I acknowledge their change in manner could be down to many different things and not necessarily anything to do with being part of a blended family.

If you were to think about life before, some of the things that you may be experiencing now are no different to what happened previously, it's just this time the dimensions have changed and perhaps unconditional love is proving a bit tricky and testing (to say the least)…!

***

I will be 'going-on' about communication throughout this book. It really is not to be underestimated, not to be pushed to one side, 'Oh we can talk about that later', or 'I haven't got time right now' – seriously get your communication lines opened up, even if it does feel like you haven't got time or could be late for something. These conversations are important enough for that person to bring it up. Be kind, patient and hear what they have to say (8.2). You do not and are not expected to have all the answers.

Wherever you see numbers in a bracket, for example (7.1), this refers to another section in the book, which has further information on the subject that I have referred to in that text.

***

When working with clients as a counsellor, I explore many

different ways of how my client could communicate their needs, and together we both recognise the first way may not always work.

I remember one client who really wanted their dad to hear them and, in the end, after trying out a variety of different methods, texting was the way to go. The dad felt it gave him time to process what the other person was saying, without feeling that they had to respond immediately. If the first attempt or what you may feel is the most obvious method of communication (for you) doesn't succeed try and try again. Remember, everyone is themselves, so you may use different methods for different members of your family.

I personally think the previous paragraph could work wonders for all manner of relationships, be it friends, family, work colleagues or intimate relationships – just putting it out there.

***

Before we go any further, I would like you to imagine this for me (I did say I'm a visual person.)

Imagine, you are going to London. You know that is what you are going to do and it is not a surprise. You have planned and prepared and you know the day and time that you are going to London. You have decided, that you are going to get there by train, you have already worked out if there are any changes, where to catch the train from and how long it will roughly take. You may have even bought the tickets. You may have looked at what restaurants and places of interest to visit and which hotel to stay. You are already imagining the relief of getting there and being carefree for a few days…

Due to logistics, your child is joining you two thirds of the way through your train journey. All they know is, that they are joining you on the train. You may have been getting ready for your London trip for some time. For your child however this is the first time they have heard about it. They may have already had plans for this evening or coming weekend. For them, they are now playing 'catch-up'.

What I am trying to explain here is that you will be steps ahead when it comes to separation or meeting a new partner. For your child, they will be playing 'catch-up', as they possibly won't be privy to your thoughts and plans. They may not have been aware that you and your partner were at the end of your relationship or that you were dating (if that's a 'thing' anymore) let alone serious about another person.

I totally appreciate that when things may feel tough, or tougher than normal, remember what station you got on, and what train station your child got on. Just like the film *Sliding Doors* everything is the same but different.

***

One last thing, when I refer to a child in this book, I mean any child that you have irrelevant of age. A child could be a toddler, an adolescent, a young adult or an adult. I really need you to make this connection that your child or stepchild of whatever age is still 'the child' in the situations that you will go through.

You will always be their parent no matter what age, and that is exactly the same but for them being the child. Yes, there will be times for instance when they are young adults and wished to be treated like young adults, but on the whole remember who is the child and who is the parent in this relationship going forward. (Even though there will probably be times when you might want to throw yourself on the floor and have a full-on tantrum – that's fine you can do that, but you are still the adult in the relationship.)

Oh, and one more thing. This book is in no way about blaming or pointing fingers, it is purely to help a blended family through the many pitfalls that 'nuclear' families go through, but because they are nuclear families the ramifications tend not to feel so catastrophic! (Or possibly they do!)

This book is really about being true to you and being the best that you can be. It also offers suggestions and communication methods that could be used to encourage the other family members to be the best that they can be in this new family.

The great thing is, you're reading this book, which means you've not given up. Instead you are looking to find an alternative way to navigate this new area.

Good luck you are doing great already!

Sophie

Welcome to Holland

I was working with a couple who told me about the story of Holland. The idea stayed with me long after the session, which lead me to *Googling* it. As I read it, I totally got how it related to that couple. Furthermore it made me think even more about how the essay can resonate in so many areas, including blended families.

I couldn't find the exact link to this essay, but I do agree with what 'bumblebee' said about it in her post on 4th September 2009… "It is a good way of helping family members understanding how they may be experiencing such a confusing and emotional time…'

"Welcome to Holland"
By Emily Perl Kingsley, 1987. All rights reserved.

I am often asked to describe the experience of raising a child with a disability – to try to help people who have not shared that unique experience to understand it, to imagine how it would feel. It's like this…

When you're going to have a baby, it's like planning a fabulous vacation trip – to Italy. You buy a bunch of guidebooks and make your wonderful plans. The Colosseum. Michelangelo's David. The gondolas in Venice. You may learn some handy phrases in Italian. It's all very exciting.

After months of eager anticipation, the day finally arrives. You pack your bags and off you go. Several hours later, the plane lands. The stewardess comes in and says, "Welcome to Holland."

"Holland?!?" you say. "What do you mean Holland?? I signed up for Italy! I'm supposed to be in Italy. All my life I've dreamed of going to Italy."

But there's been a change in the flight plan. They've landed in Holland and there you must stay. The important thing is that they haven't taken you to a horrible, disgusting, filthy place, full of pestilence, famine and disease. It's just a different place. So you must go out and buy new guidebooks. And you must learn a whole new language. And you will meet a whole new group of people you would never have met.

It's just a different place. It's slower-paced than Italy, less flashy than Italy. But after you've been there for a while and you catch your breath, you look around... and you begin to notice that Holland has windmills... and Holland has tulips. Holland even has Rembrandts.

But everyone you know is busy coming and going from Italy... and they're all bragging about what a wonderful time they had there. And for the rest of your life, you will say "Yes, that's where I was supposed to go. That's what I had planned."

And the pain of that will never, ever, ever, ever go away... because the loss of that dream is a very, very significant loss. But... if you spend your life mourning the fact that you didn't get to Italy, you may never be free to enjoy the very special, the very lovely things.... about Holland.

1. You Are Not Alone

I won't know the reason for you reading this book. The chance is that things are perhaps not going as well as you had hoped, or it could be that your situation has dramatically changed.

You may be encompassing many different feelings about the break up in your relationship and feel unsure of who you can turn to. On the other hand, you may feel thoroughly fed up going over what feels like the same story, time and time again.

Whilst right now, you may feel lonely or alone in this situation, I would like you to acknowledge *how* you are feeling, but also reassure you that you will be ok and things will improve.

However you are feeling – ashamed, hopeless, disillusioned, angry or in despair, to name a few, taking a few moments to create a list of support options during these times could benefit you greatly.

Support options could be family or friends; these people may be able to help for specific areas that you may wish to share and talk about. There may be the 'dynamic-lets-get-things-done-friend', or the 'you-can-be-sad-with-me-friend' or the 'I'll-help-take-your-mind-off-things-friend' and not forgetting the 'cook-a-meal-and-have-a glass-of-wine-or-two-friend'.

Let each person know what role you need them to play, when you contact them. By giving them the heads-up, it could feel easier reaching out to them, and also they will know what is required of them instead of guessing what you might need and potentially getting it wrong. This will not be helpful for either of you.

If you would prefer to talk to someone, who doesn't know you or your situation, someone whom you won't feel judged by or the need for you to censor how it is for you right now, there are options:

a) your GP could refer you for '*Time to Talk*' for free time-limited counselling.

b) you could arrange private counselling: word of mouth or the *Counselling Directory* are good places to start, along with searching the internet for counsellors in your area.

c) talk to the *Samaritans* – contrary to popular belief, you haven't got to be suicidal to talk to the *Samaritans* and one of the many positives, is that they are available 24/7 – T: 116123 or E: jo@samaritans. org (UK)

1.1. Do what's right for YOU!

I am very aware as I write that heading your response to that could be so different to other people's responses. These may include; "If I did what was right for me I wouldn't be in this 'mess'" or "Yeah right, if only it was that easy!"

When I say, "Do what's right for you," I mean as of now. If you have spoken to people about what is happening in your relationship, I am pretty certain that people are more than happy to share, what *they* would do if they were in your position/situation. The key word there is *if*, because they are not in *your* position and even if they were in a *similar* situation in the past, they are also not you.

No one actually knows, what it may feel like to be you. No one has walked in your shoes throughout your relationship. By all means you may choose to speak to certain friends for example, who may help you vent off your feelings and give you space to slate your Ex. There is nothing wrong in that, if that is what you need at that moment in time.

When we look at what's right for you, there could be many different areas that this is linked to. To make it a bit easier for you, like an onion, let's peel back the layers, let's look at these 'layers' one-by-one.

Let's say, that you have either decided to call an end to your relationship, or your partner has just ended it. As hard as this may seem, first of all what are the day-to-day things, which may need your attention immediately?

For instance, who normally does the school run? Does one parent do the morning and the other do the evening, or do you/they do both, due to either of your working hours?

Is this arrangement still possible to continue with or is the parent moving out of the area? Could there be anyone else who can help? This also ties in with (2.1) and telling work. There may be the option to do flexible working hours, or you could potentially work from home. As an alternative option, does the school have an afterschool club, which can facilitate keeping your child longer at the end of each day?

Can you see what we are doing here? I am very aware that, understandably your mind will be pinging off in all directions, trying to make sense of what has happened. You are reliving the past few months/years trying to work out where it all went wrong, or racing ahead to the future. Where will you and the child live and how about your financial situation and we will come to that.

Right now, whilst you are in the process of making sense of it all, getting some of the basics in place could help relieve you of added worries and, as odd as this may seem, enable you to have some form of normality/control in your day-to-day life.

With the school run sorted(ish), if possible write down a list of other areas that realistically need more immediate attention i.e. sleeping arrangements. If a parent is moving out, are you able to 'share' the same bedroom just while you clear some grey areas up? If you have a spare room and before the parent moves into that room, it could be very helpful now telling your child the true reason why – (2.1); this is *really* important and not to be overlooked.

As much as I appreciate that it may feel less than ideal, a parent does not move into the spare room before you have told your child. Should your child be used to seeing them in that bedroom i.e. one parent works shifts and hence sleeps in that room so as to not wake the other parent up, then this will not seem to be unusual for them.

The reason for the parent not moving into the spare room until you have spoken to your child is because, whether we may feel uncomfortable, children work better with the truth. If their parent were to move into the spare room and their child is told it is because mummy has a cold and is keeping daddy awake, the realisation will be that the move into the spare room was actually because their parents are splitting up and that they had been lied to.

Their world has had this sudden rupture (remember the train and them playing catch-up). Which for them *(being told mummy had a cold and therefore is sleeping in the spare room)*, began as a lie.

We need children to feel safe and secure, and their parents are instrumental in building this secure base. Lies make our base insecure. Our base is our foundation and we need it to be as solid as it can be, in order to stay strong for any other of life's challenges that are met along the way, now and in the future.

If on the other hand a parent often uses the spare room, because they snore etc., then using the room will not seem out of the ordinary. However children will pick up if the parent is spending longer periods of time in that room than previously – children are very observant!

You may feel that you need to take time out to work out what to do. Maybe go and spend some time at a friends or family members house, before any changes are made. That's absolutely fine, just remember to communicate with your child what you are doing, reassure them that you will be back (particularly if they are not used to you going away).

Make arrangements to call them at a certain time or times each day. Having set times could potentially make it easier for you. Any 'difficult or awkward' conversations with your now Ex, could take place before or after those calls with your child.

This way your child will hopefully not be exposed to any residue of your feelings following *those* conversations.

I know I say that it is important for children to see parents cry or upset, but preferably not when they are on the phone or away from their parent, as this could cause them to be anxious and afraid of what is happening.

It may be, that you would prefer your partner to go away for a few days and again, talk this through with them, as to how they will continue maintaining contact with their child.

You may feel that you want your partner gone and all their belongings and anything that reminds you of them to be removed from your home. Whilst that may feel right for you that may not initially be helpful for your child to witness. As the effect of one minute having both parents and then only one and no trace of the other, could stifle conversations for your child to have about the parent that is no longer living with them.

Removing all traces could feel like they never existed and yes that may be how you're feeling (and I'm aware this part is about doing what's right for you), but there could also be a greater impact for the wider family.

You can of course write a list or imagine in your mind their things no longer being there. Buying new bed linen and having your bedroom redecorated could, to start with, be another way of managing 'cleansing' them out of your life. I totally get that you are hurting and that you are not going to want to continue to feel that pain.

As I said, there will almost likely be plenty of advice giving from friends, family and work colleagues, but just because it's advice, that doesn't necessarily make it good, logical or indeed the right advice for you. On the other hand, you may have a friend that tends to infuriate you because they always look at things logically and maybe now is the time that friend could help and support you?

Maybe nothing makes sense and you have no idea which way to turn. Here counselling could be an option. Whilst you may feel backed into a corner with what has happened, doing what is right for you is about you taking back some control. Not in a manipulative way, but in a constructive way for *you*.

1.2. Hindsight is a wonderful thing!

Hindsight: "Understanding of a situation or event only after it has happened or developed."

Yep, that little word that doesn't quite bite you on the bum, but definitely taps you on the shoulder in a kind of 'told you so way' – not that you need reminding. You may have wished at times for hindsight in the past. However, your friends may have hindsight, which could benefit you now.

Of course, I am not expecting you to having developed hindsight in your new situation. As you haven't had any hindsight moments, friends and relatives who may have been in similar situations, could contribute.

This section is about research. (Don't groan hear, or is that how *I* feel about research?!) Here, you are gathering information, fact finding and getting 'comfortable' or familiar with the situation that you now find yourself in. I appreciate comfortable could be a difficult word to swallow right now, or use in this context.

I am by no means saying your friends and relatives are experts and that you are not, but what I am saying is, as part of your 'research', ask them when they have been in a similar situation to you, what worked and what didn't work.

Even if they only come up with one thing, that's still one thing for you to note down. If they are comfortable in doing so, ask them what happened that led to whatever it was that worked or didn't work – like I said they are not experts, but hearing what they have been through could prove helpful, insightful or perhaps even thought-provoking.

Let's do another visualisation; imagine that you are going on holiday to Venice, and a friend has been once or several times. Would you ask them their top tips on what to do, or not to do, or would you 'fend' for yourself?

If you decided to fend for yourself, why would you do that? Who knows, they might know a great restaurant or gondolier tip, or the best time to visit a place of interest or indeed a different time to visit it.

I remember reading a blog about someone seeing Venice in the early hours of the morning, and I mean early like 5 am (that is early for me). Personally I couldn't imagine getting up that early on a holiday, but apparently Venice at that time of the morning is serene and quite majestic by all accounts.

Although I'm not planning on going to Venice as we speak, I must have read that article at least over a year ago. It has however stayed in my mind, and if I was to visit Venice, I may just be tempted one morning to test the early hours of Venice myself! Yes, even I might set the alarm clock to see Venice at 5 am!

So you see, this is how other people's experiences can help you view things from a different perspective. Why not say that you would like to ask them what they in hindsight would have done differently, when they went through their separation. Like the early morning in Venice your friends and relatives will almost definitely have 'hindsight' moments, which could be tripping off of their tongues!

You may never use their knowledge, but like the 'early morning in Venice' it will sit there in the archives of your brain, available should a similar situation come up. I'm not expecting you to remember everything, it may even be a key word that triggers your archives in which case, you can contact your friend or relative, and ask them to remind you of what happened.

I seem to be referring a lot to Italy, but just like Rome wasn't built in day, you are not going to have all the blocks in place to manage what is happening. But with a bit of research, this could help you on your way. Or at the very least, if you are able to do so, you can see how far your friends have come since their situation that they are sharing with you.

You may be thinking, that you don't know where to start or what to ask. Here I would suggest that you write down your fears – eek!! Write down what it is, that you are really afraid of. This may feel a bit like 'tempting fate'.

My clients look mortified when I acknowledge that they are doing well, as if suddenly all their hard work is going to become undone, but it's not, of course it's not, but the fear is there.

Just like your fears, once you say them out loud the power is literally taken away. As soon as we admit something to ourselves, we may find that we feel potentially more in control than by allowing our fears to hide in the dark crevices of our minds.

The important thing is that everyone has fears, and everyone is worried about not succeeding, or lacking confidence, or not being good enough, or something or other. What we need to do, is look at *your* fears. They are not silly or stupid, they are very real, and this is where we start removing their power. Once you have either said them out loud or written them down, you will now be able to tackle them, one-by-one.

Even the thought of acknowledging your fears may feel quite overwhelming, that's ok, do it in steps. First of all say to yourself that at some point, you are going to acknowledge your fears in your head – that can be enough for now.

When you have recognised your fears, imagine a snow globe, where we have shaken the fears away from the bottom, and now we are going to let them settle back down again. This is for you, not for your fears, this is for you to acclimatise yourself to knowing that you are going to take on your fears.

Ok, when you feel slightly more comfortable, I would then like you to tell yourself, that you are going to say them out loud, maybe one at a time, or just count how many there are. Can you see how by breaking these down into bite-size pieces, it makes the fears more digestible and hopefully not overwhelming. Besides I am sitting right next to you as you do this, you are not alone.

Each time you move closer to writing them down, give yourself time to readjust. This is really important, because fears are scary and acknowledging our fears can feel even scarier. I mean who likes feeling vulnerable or scared?

As you get used to saying the fears out loud or mulling them over in your mind, you may begin to feel more comfortable asking a friend or relative if they were afraid of 'X fear', or you might ask them what were they afraid of at first, so you can then be reassured that they too had their own fears.

Remember your fears are NOT silly – they are your fears and we need to respect that's how you feel.

The important part about this chapter, is looking after you. If you are able to do research, then do it, as the good ole saying goes, 'Knowledge is power'.

If you feel unsure where to start and you feel able to do so, speak to your child's school. Ask them what they have noticed helped and didn't help when a child's family has separated or blended. Of course they won't share confidential data or name the child or their family, but they may say X helped or Y didn't. They may have suggestions that you hadn't considered. (*Google* isn't the only place to find information.)

I do fully appreciate this may be new territory for you, it may feel like a complete foreign land and a foreign language being spoken (like the essay Holland [pg.15], particularly if solicitors have got involved.

However, what I am hoping this chapter may offer is reassurance that you are not on your own and indeed you do not need to be on your own.

Let me leave this chapter with this last thought, "If the shoe was on the other foot, how would you yourself feel about a friend or relative asking you about your hindsight?"

2. Separating

So, one of you has made the decision that it is time to break up your relationship/separate. For both of you this will probably not be easy, whether you are the one to say those words, or you are the one on the receiving end of those words.

I totally understand there will be an array of emotions and questions, or maybe no questions but potentially demands for one of the parents to leave the family home. You may want them to 'get out' whilst you make sense of what has just happened or happening. Cortisol will be running through your body to help get you through the next minutes, hours and days.

Whilst this may feel like the hardest thing to do, it could be really beneficial for you both to sit down and discuss how this decision will be shared with your child.

If necessary, I wonder if there is a friend who could act as a mediator to enable you and your now Ex to work through this incredibly painful time. Talking to your partner right now might be the last thing on your mind as you could be wishing yourself as far away as possible from them. Or for that matter that this wasn't happening.

Potentially you are able to be amicable – there is no right or wrong, because they are your feelings and so that makes them right. I'm not saying to act on your feelings but to acknowledge them.

Whichever place you are in, the conversations that will start taking place need to be 'child' conscious. What I mean by that, is your child will notice or sense that something isn't quite right. (That is if they haven't witnessed the exchange of words that have ended up in you separating.)

So, how do you go about this? Conversations to friends may become hushed voices on the phone or behind closed doors. Where possible, try to have these conversations when your child is not around, or ensure your child is distracted long enough for you to be able to talk. Asking your child to leave the room, or saying you want some 'adult time' could make them feel vulnerable and more anxious about what is going on.

I do appreciate I am writing a book and real life doesn't always happen like this. When you are able to adapt your conversations to be 'child conscious', this could well provide you with the space and time you need and your child with the reassurance they need.

Children have the most amazing creative imaginations, so in this situation, try not to provide them with opportunities to fill the gaps with their imagination.

2.1. HELP! We are splitting up

I feel one of the most important things, is for you both to be a unit with how the situation will unfold. I totally understand that could be a tall order right now and the last thing you want to do is to be in the same room as your partner, let alone 'work together'.

What and how to tell your child would benefit from taking some time and consideration to decide what you are going to say. If being in the same room is an absolute no-no, then both of you saying the same thing but at separate times is vital. Ideally word-for-word.

Children don't need to be told all the sordid details, or hear one parent punishing the other. On the whole most children, in an ideal filmmaking world, would like their parents to stay together.

Depending on the age of your child, they may have; a) no idea; b) been aware that their parents seem to be 'a bit' unhappy (that was me); c) been incredibly aware that their parents are unhappy or d) preferred their parents not to be together.

Telling the children – When speaking to your child, I appreciate there isn't a 'best time' but where possible speak to them, when they have time to process what you have said. This could be at the weekend so they have time to 'adjust' before school on Monday, or a school holiday is coming up so that could be more helpful?

Give them the opportunity to ask questions, and should you end up crying, that is both understandable and acceptable. Too many parents 'protect' their children from seeing them sad, why? Crying is incredibly natural, and it helps educate children that it is ok to cry, such as if your child gets upset or says "But won't daddy be lonely on their own?"

This is really important not to dismiss their feelings or comments and say they are being silly and "Of course daddy will be fine." As we talked about your feelings previously, these are their feelings and they are very real and are definitely not silly, the same as your feelings are real and not silly either.

Your child may say things that create a strong negative reaction i.e. your child says, "I want mummy to still read me my bedtime story." You may be thinking "Well that's not going to happen!"

In this instance, you don't have to answer them straight away, you could say "That's a really good question" or "I can hear you still want mummy to read you a bedtime story and mummy and daddy will think about that." This will show your child that you *heard* them (8.2).

A suggestion could be, that two nights of the week to start with, the parent returns back to your child's home and reads them their story. Yes this may be uncomfortable for you, but think about how comforting and reassuring your child may find it.

You are not expected to know all the answers, so it's ok to write your child's question(s) down and come back to them – even if your immediate thought in your head is 'I don't want my Ex coming back into my home!'

Telling the family and friends – You may have already told some family members and friends, or if the breakup has come as a surprise to you, then possibly not.

But before you do speak to them, if you feel able to do so, think about what you might need from these people over the next few weeks. We looked previously at 'support options'.

For a friend it might mean picking your child up from school and having them a couple of hours whilst you're still at work two evenings a week. Without realising it, you could have a whole pool of resources right at your fingertips.

The thought of repeating yourself and 'reliving' your situation may feel overwhelming, and you might not want to keep feeling those feelings. That is totally understandable, and so you could ask a sibling to tell some family members or a friend to speak to your other friends.

You may even decide to communicate to a group of people, for example using *WhatsApp*, along with explaining what you need from them right now. How you choose to do this is ok. You may feel you 'should' (15.1) tell people face-to-face, but do you know what, if that's too hard for you right now, then it's probably not the right way for you and like I said, that is completely ok.

Telling Work – Divorce is one of the top three most stressful things a person/persons can go through, so do not feel that you have to take this challenge on your own.

Speak to your manager or Human Resources/Personnel, or college tutor. You may feel a crushing shame of what has happened and are trying to work out 'what you did wrong' or 'where did it all go wrong'. Knowing other people are now looking out for you, knowing you have that 'go to' person, when you're having a wobbly day can be a real lifesaver.

Telling the school – Definitely let your child's school know what is happening. When I say telling the school, yes this does extend to sixth form, college and university.

Do ask them what pastoral or student support is available for your child. Just because your child might be older, doesn't mean they need support any less. In fact, if they are in education away from home, they may need it more.

The school can look out for signs of your child being in distress or not coping. Their behaviours may change good or bad – suddenly they may want to overly please the teachers or become disruptive – both of which are understandable.

Also discuss emergency contact details. I was 'banned' from being on the list due to the Ex wanting to punish my partner. But they were indirectly punishing their children too.

I remember the discomfort of both of my parents going to parents evening when they were together, they not only looked disgruntled about going but also looked completely unconnected. It hardly looked like a joyous occasion for them even if it was for my siblings' education and me

I realise now, that it was nothing to do with what my teachers said about me, which was generally that I talked too much! So imagine what it could have looked like if they had had to attend parents evening separately, they would have looked like fish out of water!

Fast-forward to my blended family…

As I mention throughout the book, I had a good relationship with my youngest stepchild, and when it was their parents evening, they begged me to come along. Reason being they were incredibly excited to introduce me to their friends, not that I was aware of that at the time.

This is where we need to give children credit, my youngest stepchild had already spoken to the school about the complex family issues and the relationship between their parents was very acrimonious.

The arrangements were made so that their mother had the early slot, and we had the last slot of the evening. The two separate and well-spaced slots were very helpful, albeit ours was incredibly late! Their parent and I spoke to the teachers, and I was introduced to all of their friends, which I could then appreciate was of great importance to them. So as you can see, it did work.

It only got tricky when it became apparent over the coming months that our youngest was incredibly unhappy at school.

On our week, when they returned home from school, they often came in crying and really didn't want to go back to school.

We looked at what was happening for them, and obviously there was more to it. I shall not bore you with the full story, however together my stepchild, their parent and I discussed other school options.

Unfortunately the idea of my youngest stepchild changing schools went down like a lead balloon, and was deemed totally unacceptable by my partners Ex for some reason or other. What became apparent was the fact that I was involved in talking through with my stepchild about what could be a better school choice for them.

This is where it can get incredibly difficult with blended families. This is where the adults no matter what their feelings are about the other partners or Exes, somehow need to learn to work together when it comes to the children.

Yes, you may feel that you 'know what's best' for your child, however children can be incredibly restrained in only showing you whatever they feel you *want* to see or know. Or indeed what they feel you can take on right now.

There will be other future engagements whereby your child may want you both to attend or may not, due to how uncomfortable that may feel for your child or others.

I completely understand if being in the same room with your Ex is an absolute no-go, that is ok. However, you will need to explain this to your child so that they understand it isn't them, that you are saying no to, but the proposition of being in the same room as your Ex.

I know someone well, who was pretty much bullied throughout their whole relationship and during the divorce and beyond. Basically this went on until the children became adults and no further contact was necessary between the two parents. Even now, if they were to be expected to be at the same event as their Ex, this would cause the person anxiety and ensuing panic attacks, both of which are detrimental to their mental health.

We never truly know or may even be able to understand the magnitude of what goes on in a relationship. There will be times when parents, siblings or others, may not be able to be in the same room or at a function.

Whilst I understand, what you are being asked to attend could be significant i.e. a graduation, wedding, christening involving your child, you may not be able to be part of that ceremony. This to me is fully acceptable, as you are simply exercising self-care. The hardest bit for your child will be to understand your decision, and accept ideally with grace.

2.2. Help! We're splitting up – AGAIN

I totally accept, that you may be thinking, "You have already read about splitting up/separating, why are you talking about it again?" And yes, I agree with you, I have. However the difference is this is *again* and believe me there probably will be some differences.

Breaking up or separating again, does not mean it will be exactly the same – let's be honest, no two relationships are the same, so why would splitting up again be any different?

I am also acutely aware that you may be feeling even less happy going through it again and indeed the very fact that it *has* happened again. I am not saying you should (15.1), but you could be feeling a sense of shame or failure.

The reason that I raise these feelings is that in order to 'cover up' your potential feelings of shame/failure, you may skip over certain parts or even 'gloss' over them – but just like hindsight (1.2) it could come back and 'bite you on the bum' – so as much as I acknowledge your pain, please try not to skip this even if you feel we have already covered it.

I agree, there are still the same points; telling the children, telling friends and family, telling work and telling school (college or uni). However there could also be other elements.

A relationship takes a lot of work, we may think finding a new partner and getting into a relationship was hard enough!

Yet, you are now aiming for an 'interdependent' relationship; a relationship where partners can rely on each other but also maintain their autonomous identity. Along with all its regular challenges alongside the blended family challenges can sometimes feel like trawling through treacle.

So, back to the here and now. One of the areas that we didn't look at previously, is looking at the impact of separating when there are children from both sides involved.

For some/one child they could be 'relieved' to not have to 'put up' with the stepsiblings anymore. However, another child may have formed a strong attachment and definitely does not want to be separated from them, let alone not have them in their life going forward.

As discussed previously, it is really important to clearly and honestly communicate what is happening with your child. Again, give your child the space and time for them to explore what this new news means to them. You are not expecting them to have thought everything through, particularly if they have just learned about it.

Like the previous chapter, they may immediately have questions; "Does that mean I can have X's room?" or "Are we still all going on holiday together?" Remember, you do not need to have all the answers, just calmly acknowledge what your child has just asked and let them know you will think about it. If possible, give a timescale.

You may have not even thought about the next part of your life not involving your now Ex, let alone their child. Or, you may be feeling wretched about not having their child in your life going forward.

Your child may have built a strong bond with your Ex's parents. Your child may not have any biological grandparents alive or in their lives. All of these strings of relationships, will need to be looked at – tentatively.

This may or may not seem a bit weird, but bear with me. Your Ex, may have a pet that will be leaving with them too. Again, consider the impact that may have. Your child may have walked the dog after school, or they used to cuddle up with the pet whilst watching TV. Now, I am not saying that you have to rush out and replace said pet, but again, to be aware that this will also be another loss to your child.

These are the main areas that can differ from (2.1).

3. Living arrangements

So you now find yourself potentially looking at shared custody of your child. I say potentially, as that might not be an option, because your Ex may have become estranged, a court order has been made, or adaptions made due to your child being at risk.

You may have already planned how you see it working in your head, or what you are prepared to do, but as per previous chapters, it is important for you to keep your views to yourself just for the time being.

My idea is as follows: first of all, write down your potential suggestions for how you see the living arrangements being played out. I would then like you to write down your emotions behind your possible thoughts.

Be really honest with yourself, do you want to punish your Ex, have they got a new partner and you feel angry, hurt, or confused and don't want your child to have a replacement mum or dad? Or worst still, have a 'ready-made family' like you all used to be?

I am fully aware that this will stir up a lot of emotions, however I do feel this could be really helpful in the long term, even though it may feel incredibly painful for you to do right now.

Once you have completed this, I would like you to do something good for you, perhaps make yourself a coffee, go for a walk, have a hot bath, watch your favourite TV programme. Whatever it is that will take you back to feeling in a better place – we are now looking at trying to 'settle' you, settle the emotions that have just been revisited.

You may find that you are able to go back to your list in a different frame of mind, or you may choose to leave it a few days. People can change their mind, which particularly in this instance can be really helpful. Therefore if you find yourself able to revisit the possibilities and allow yourself to be more open-minded about what *could* happen, this prevents any decisions being set in stone.

Your child's age could affect the suggestions also. Depending on their age, they may very likely have their own opinion on this matter as it does massively affect them. Section (3.2) looks into this in more detail.

However you feel about the possibility of not living with your child full time, please try to be 'child conscious' and not share these feelings with your child; "How sad mummy/ daddy will be, when they go back to stay at their other parent's house". That will not be helpful to all parties, both parents, any new partners and most importantly your child.

3.1. Maintain or make a relationship with your child

You may find a chapter on having a relationship with your child seems a bit bizarre. However go with it.

I once worked with a mum and child, sometimes together and sometimes separately. The mum thought they had a good relationship and on the whole they did.

Through counselling the child started to feel more comfortable and able to explore their relationship with their mum. They felt the other siblings affected or imposed on this relationship, there never seemed to be any time where no one else was around. What transpired, was that the child craved 5–10 minutes a day for themselves and their mum.

You may be thinking to yourself "Really, 5–10 minutes?" or whatever judgement you jumped to. However yes, 5–10 minutes was vitally important for this young person. For me, I would say well done to them for recognising what they felt they needed.

The time that they wanted was to talk about maybe nothing in particular, definitely not to be used for being told-off or 'nagged'. Instead this was protected child/parent time. The mum, initially surprised by their child's request, soon appreciated how having that time with their child enabled their relationship to blossom further.

The mum also recognised that when she had previously been communicating with her child, it was generally to complain about something they hadn't done. So for the mum too, it was nice to have some quality time to enjoy each other's company.

This illustrates the importance of giving your child dedicated time, to listen to what they feel is important to them. *(Even if it doesn't seem important to you.)* I hear this a lot when I work with young people how they would like some time with their parent.

Parents often say to me that their child is always on their phone or tablet, yet lots of children share with me how they feel the same about their parents always being on *their* devices.

I am by no means saying all men are alpha male or being sexist or whatever other equality or ism that you want to throw at me. It can go the other way too, which I will explain in a bit.

But let's say your child's dad is really into rugby and so therefore encourages/promotes the qualities of rugby to your child, even encourages your child to play rugby. However your child is really not interested in rugby but instead likes horse riding or golf or doesn't like sport at all.

What can happen is that the parent with the interest in rugby subconsciously shows no interest in your child's other hobbies. The parent may appear dismissive to your child, which could be interpreted that they don't care or that the child's interest is not valid, or not worthy of their parents' time.

When I was at school I had no idea what I wanted to do, it was far too big a question – there's a whole world out there! So I asked my mum and she suggested for me to become a vet or a secretary, as my mum had always wanted to be a vet.

To go to Veterinary school was a no-go, as I cannot do the red stuff, even saying the word used to make me a bit squiffy.

Secretary it was then, until I later branched out myself, went to college and it all changed.

This is how easy it is for parents to pass on their own wants to their child. Therefore, it is so incredibly important to work on your relationship on an individual basis with your child. Notice the differences between them if you have more than one.

Even if you don't have a common interest, find something that you can do together. If standing by the football pitch on a Saturday morning turns you cold (literally), you could watch a movie together or go to a museum for example.

If your child is *really* into football, maybe take them to their team's football stadium for a tour, you never know you might enjoy it. Also the driving time, there and back will be protected time for the both of you. Do not underestimate the 'power' of this time and where possible try to keep devices switched off and talk or sing – together!

I remember one time after dropping my youngest stepchild off at friends and realising I still had *Justin Bieber* playing even though it wasn't necessary anymore – it did make me smile, whilst changing it to my music.

It may be that both of your children like the same team so you may take them both. But, and I use that a lot to start sentences, make time to see your children as individuals.

Our middle son, yep the one that I didn't see eye-to-eye with in the beginning, loved skateboarding and doing tricks. He would set up his ramp and various other things to jump off or on to and then would ask someone to watch him do his tricks.

Well you may imagine, I wasn't really keen, as I had such a strong sense of him not really liking me. He did however want someone to watch and I acknowledged, skateboarding was his thing although definitely not mine!

However, I appeared to be the only one available, and so I did. I watched him do his tricks until it was too dark to see. Sometimes we would move from the back garden to the front, so that I could continue watching and congratulating him on his moves, under the glow of our security lights.

Having worked at our relationship together, it has fully blossomed, just like the mum and child at the beginning of this chapter and we now sit very comfortably together talking about something and nothing.

We both love live concerts but have mainly different tastes in music and yet it is a joy to share how the event was. We are both keen to exercise and often talk about the latest obstacle race that he has entered. Where possible I would either turn up and surprise him and his friends, or make arrangements to meet him at the end to congratulate him on taking part and making sure he's ok too.

I will never forget the first time his dad and I appeared. There were hundreds of cyclists and I had roughly worked out what time he would be at a water stop. So, armed with energy bars and drinks, we took off. The picture on his face was truly wonderful – he was noticed and we had gone out of our way to cheer him on.

I am certainly not trying to be stepparent of the year, I have totally let myself down at times, but then again, I didn't have the tools, patience and knowledge that I do now (or this book).

Yes, if I could go back and change things, erase glaringly bad mistakes and judgements on my part I would. But what I am hoping to show you is that it takes two and sometimes a little more effort on the part of one person to spark up this interest. Like any other relationship it takes commitment and investment.

Think about your own friends that you are really keen to see. If they cancel for whatever reason, remember how you feel, or, when you do see them and they ask you questions about what you have been up to, how their interest in you makes you feel valued.

You may have a child and they haven't, but they still ask how they are getting on and I am aware that it feels nice, that they thought about them and therefore show you, that you are important to them and they value you.

As with friendships we can allow them to drift off and lose contact, but as a parent, this really should not be an option, even subconsciously. I think it is a privileged role, I accept the word privileged may not be the first word to trip off of your tongue and at times, I didn't feel very privileged – *but it is*. So where possible, show them that you are interested in them, show them that you do think about them.

Let me give you an example. You may hear that their favourite football team is doing really well and sending them a text saying how well they are doing will go down a storm – yes really!

The last bit about maintaining or making a relationship with your child is about doing this even if they don't get on with your partner. Do not force your child or partner to like each other.

I for example did not like my dad's new wife at all and as a result of that, my dad allowed our relationship to become estranged. I desperately wanted to see him and voiced this to my other siblings. In turn they spoke to my dad and his response was that if I wanted to see him, I had to see him with his wife! Wow, I certainly wasn't heard or felt considered.

I repeat do not, ever put your child in that situation, or your new partner.

What I feel could really work, is having a relationship with your child and over time they may want to meet up with you and your partner or indeed your partner maybe ready to meet with them – but absolutely no forcing (10.2)!

Like I said in the beginning, this may seem bizarre, but a) I have had this first hand and b) I have worked with many clients, who felt forced to accept their parents partner or indeed feel that they were unable to have 1:1 time with their parent.

Remember we are all individual and not every size fits all.

3.2. Your child and their homes

In this section, we will look more closely at shared parenting with your child.

Please note, that I am in no way telling you how to divide your child between the two of you. I am also acutely aware, that for many reasons there sometimes isn't the option for your child to stay or indeed visit the other parent.

For the sake of this chapter, let us assume that there is the possibility of splitting their time between the two of you. I would like you to focus on the word possibility, which suggests that nothing is set in stone. There is room for movement and indeed space to explore how your child may feel about this.

As acknowledged previously, you may have your reasons needing to have some 'time-out' from you child, or you feel that the other parent is 'shirking' their responsibility regarding shared custody of your child.

However your views on this subject really must be aired with adults only, this does not include your child even if they are legally classed as adults. It is not helpful to either party to learn of your disgruntlements.

All this does is reiterate the potential disjointed view they may already have in that they are not wanted or that they are a plain nuisance.

So back to the task in hand... Grab a pen and a piece of paper.

Write down the various possible options available. What could the shared parenting look like realistically, thinking of your situation and what you know of your Ex's current arrangements?

Again, the word here is current. We are not looking into the future as things can change but instead what is the situation like right now. At this stage you are looking at it from your point of view and how much you feel your Ex *may be* able to do.

The next stage is to consider your child's view. What do you think they may like to do? Again, we are *playing* with these ideas, you don't actually know how they feel.

I remember my sister and I talking as adults and her saying how at the time of our parents' divorce, she had decided she wanted to live with my dad. If I am to be honest, I never saw *that* coming.

I had always assumed we would all live with our mum. I asked her what had changed her mind and she explained that she had been gearing herself up to tell our mum, knowing that she may be a little upset.

In the meantime, our mum who was completely unaware of sis' thoughts, had said during a particularly difficult day, "At least I've got you." So that was that, my sister's fate was sealed, she felt she no longer could do what she had wanted.

This is another illustration of how one comment can change a path so easily and not necessarily for the better.

Could you consider if your level of communication with your Ex would allow a joint approach, to look at the options available with regard to the sharing? I appreciate the outcome *could* be depending on the age of your child although do not necessarily assume this.

Before sharing your ideas with your child, I would suggest asking your child to write down what *they* may like to do, please give them time and space and absolutely no hints as to your ideas or opinions on this matter. Be aware of what you may want them to do and indeed what you may think is right for them due to their age.

Remember, a lot of the time children want to please or not upset their parents and they may say you can decide. I would still strongly urge you to encourage them to think about it and say that you will speak to them about it in a few days. (Give them a specific day here and make a note of it in your diary or on your phone).

Once your child has had the opportunity to think about this, sit down together and share the options that you came up with. Again, notice their reactions or comments (you may want to write their reactions down to be able to refer back to) but ideally, reiterate that these are your ideas and that you would like your child time to process these options.

This way you are trying to get a holistic view which incorporates everyone's ideal. This is the starting point.

As your child get older and yours and your Ex's circumstances may change, remember to be open to alterations. Maybe on a yearly basis revisit the changeover situation.

Indeed, if your child comments on the arrangements, ask them to explain the comment in more detail to you. Do not dismiss the potential 'off the cuff' remark – there will be more to it.

Talking of 'changeover', again, without using this opportunity to 'get at' your Ex or punish them in some way. Try to make this as smooth as possible. It may mean smiling on the outside (but screaming obscenities or even crying on the inside) when pulling up outside your previous marital home or your Ex's new partners house.

Your child will pick up on what you are showing – verbal is only a small percentage of communication whereas tone and body language are so much more.

I feel the following exercise could be really helpful and if you are able to do so, please give yourself at least ten minutes. It's grab a pen and piece of paper time.

Take a moment to imagine uprooting yourself every other week or weekend.

Write down the things that you would like to take or have two columns, the other column for items or belongings you realistically wouldn't be able to take.

We all have those items we would like to take with us on holiday but don't have the space for. The difference is, this isn't a holiday for them, this, is their new way of living!

How did you feel? What did you notice about choosing what you could and could not pack? Would your items change if it was the weekend or week, or you had to take your things to school, because you were getting the bus home back to the other parents' house?

I have to say living out of a suitcase for a week or two is manageable for me. I do like the idea of a road trip but packing up my stuff every few days would drive me to distraction and so I couldn't imagine getting my head around potentially doing that every other week for what might feel like forever!

I remember us being given a list from my husband's Ex, a checklist to ensure everything was packed and returned, and the repercussions were not a consideration if they weren't! I am all too aware that 'the list' evoked strong emotions in both of us and we both felt we were being treated as children!

Ironically, Monday was changeover day for our household (we had two of the children – one week on and one week off). Mondays was also Cooking or Home Economics for my youngest stepchild, so I often waved goodbye to my kitchen items knowing, they would never be returned or seen again!

I talk about the different dynamics or rules in each home (see 4.1) and again ask you to be aware of giving your child time to adapt between the two homes. They may need a settling in period, unpacking their things, getting used to being in home 1 or home 2.

I never thought I would return to the same place on holiday (there's a whole world out there), let alone several times. Yet I have. Why, because it's easy and it's great to arrive at the hotel and within five minutes of checking-in be 'at home' with everything.

I don't know how it is for you, but when I experience a holiday, it always takes a few days to get into a routine of sorts. Unpacking and finding out meal times, or how to get into the local village or town. Usually by the end of the week, everything feels natural but then we have to pack up and go home. Imagine doing that week in, week out – ugh!

How might you react as the parent if your child realises they have left something at the other house and they need it for school tomorrow. Worse still your child knows how you might react and so just chooses to 'manage' the problem themselves at school, as that could be 'easier' than hearing about what a nuisance it might present for you.

The key thing is to make changeover as stress-free as possible. It may be on the first day back at yours, you both have your favourite pizza and watch a jointly chosen movie for instance. This small routine could help your child settle back in quicker. It is also consistent i.e. nothing immediate has changed, which will enable your child to feel safe, secure and reassured.

The other times to be considered are 'special days' such as Christmas or perhaps another religious day that your family celebrate. If possible, try to have an open discussion with your Ex about how that may look. Again, if either of you are able to do so, ask your child what their views are.

We had a situation whereby actual Danish Christmas Day was always celebrated with the children's mum for many years – this was not up for negotiation

So when many years later, their mum decided she was no longer carrying out that celebration (quite close to the event), this came as a huge surprise to us, let alone to the children. Whilst the children are all adults now, I wonder how that felt?

I appreciate what you are going through is difficult enough and you have a myriad of things to consider. When you notice these thoughts surrounding your child's two homes, write them down for you to look at when you can. At some point you could discuss these with friends and relatives about their experiences and what worked or what certainly didn't.

You haven't got to do this on your own, there could be well be a wealth of knowledge in your own support network.

3.3.   The diversity of 'changeover week'

Yes, your child moving between two homes can be as diverse as it comes. As I mentioned previously, we had my husband's eldest living with us full time and his other two children were week on week off.

Changeover day for us was 5pm on a Monday and believe me, there was no movement on that whatsoever!

If we were to look at the above arrangement, I am aware that there was never a conversation with the other two children as two why their eldest lived with their dad and indeed following on from that there was no follow-up discussion on how any of the three of them felt about living that way.

I am not saying the arrangement may have changed, although possibly one of them might have liked to change their living arrangement. But at no point were they given the opportunity to talk about how it might be for them seeing their sibling week on / week off, or indeed why they weren't living with their sibling full-time?

Indeed, it is important to acknowledge the impact for you as a parent here. How does it feel for you to be a full-time parent? Maybe if you are used to looking after your child all the time or possibly not because you worked full-time and your Ex was the main caregiver.

Again, I feel it is reasonable for you to allow yourself some time and space to notice how this arrangement may feel for you. If you would like to talk to someone about it, do speak to friends or family and not to your child. As I absolutely encourage adults to talk to adults, not children (even if your child is an adult)!

One thing for sure, is that there is no right or wrong way of 'changeover'. Yes I agree, you may have in your mind your preferences as mentioned previously however it is important to be as open-minded as you can to the variations of this.

I talk later how a client heard an adult refer to time out from their children / step-children as a 'perk' – please don't get me started on that…

I accept you may want some time out or indeed feel your Ex could be doing more, but please ensure a) you keep these thoughts to yourself or between adults and b) children are not the *5:2 diet*! They are human beings and like you and I, they are unique.

So, please, please, *please* allow yourself to consider unique and flexible 'changeover' solutions. These ideas do not have to be set-in-stone. Just like the landscape of your family has changed, your child will benefit as being recognised as an important member of the family, rather than an object passed between two homes.

3.4. Building a relationship with your stepchild

This chapter could be helpful if you feel your relationship is struggling with a stepchild.

As mentioned previously, my stepchild liked skateboarding and whilst it wasn't something I was keen on, I still encouraged him to do it and I watched him practise his skills. In the early days, it didn't necessarily bring us closer together, but it was still *time* together.

As per chapter (10.3) and the date night jar, I would like you to have a jar for your stepchild to put their suggestions in. Expect ideas that may not be enjoyable or ones that are difficult to achieve, (they are trying to make a point here). They may completely resist which is fine (for the moment – refrain from forcing the point).

The jar could also include hobbies that they like or say the name of their football team that they support. This jar, can be one of many building blocks for your relationship with your stepchild. Their ideas or hobbies that go into the jar, could provide you with ideas that you two *could,* do together.

I am saying could and not should (15.1), as again this is not about forcing your relationship. If they are not keen to write anything, ask their siblings, or if you notice something, you write it down and pop it in.

However, in the meantime, *do* (and I can't stress this enough) DO notice what foods they like and don't like. i.e. if they don't like mushrooms (my middle stepchild detested them) do your upmost to remember not to put them on their plate.

If there is a particular food that they do like, make it. If they are in their room, pop your head around the door, or text them and ask them if they would like anything such as a cup of tea. If you are going to watch a film, do not presume they won't and whilst you may prefer to not include them for your own reasons – ask them!

Yes, they will probably keep resisting you 'big time' and no, taking out mushrooms isn't a peacemaker. Through you doing these gestures is not demeaning to you (even though it may feel like it) but what it is saying, is I know you are there, I know you are struggling/hurting and yes, you do matter (even if you are being a little sod to me).

Our middle child really struggled with the divorce. Believe me when I talk about 'owning it and being the adult', there were many times that I wanted to throw myself on the floor and have the biggest adult tantrum known to mankind – however I didn't externally (but I did in my head – a lot!).

Again, I am not proud of myself but there were times when I did say things out loud, because I was also angry and hurting too. I didn't feel I could do anything right and YES I was pushed to the edge on too many occasions to remember.

During the early years, there were times when the 15-year-old angry hurting teenager inside me (from my own parents break up) reared its ugly head. We then had two teenagers (metaphorically speaking) battling it out and trying to make sense of it all – not a pretty sight I can tell you.

I am also a middle child and so again I transferred some more of my crap into the already way too big crap pile! And as you may have worked out, it continued to grow and grow.

What I feel was absolutely paramount here is that I do not feel their parents tried to understand how it was for their middle child.

Their older sibling lived with us full time, which I am sure added further confusion and questions. The youngest of the three appeared to adore me. This in the eyes of the middle child may have looked as if they were rejecting them own mum or 'siding with the enemy'.

The middle child also decided that they had to 'parent' their younger sibling and so became an 'adult' which added its own complications and emotions. It basically came to a point where we almost left them to their own devices and rarely challenged them, to try to keep peace in the home for that week.

In hindsight, I would have encouraged their dad to spend more time with them, even if they weren't behaving well or were not particularly nice to be around. I would have encouraged their Dad to take his children out without me, showing them and reassuring them, that they were important and that they did matter.

Most importantly I would have liked him to give them time and the tools in how to express what was going on for them and how they felt about the whole difficult situation. Because at times it certainly did appear to be conflicting with Team Dad and Team Mum camps and the various grenades being thrown, generally from one camp to the other.

Now during this time, fortunately their Dad and I could talk about what was going on. When we only had his eldest child living with us, it was easier and calmer. There was space for us to share, what we might be finding challenging or upsetting. However when we were back to being all five of us in the house, at times it did feel like there was no air. So what on earth could it have felt like for the sad, confused and angry middle child?

In the end this sibling decided they couldn't cope with the week on week off disruption. The two homes were worlds apart and when it came to transport we had limited buses available and at weekends this was further reduced.

At their other home they had buses galore and a train station all on their doorstep. So yes for a young teenager I can see the attraction, along with the sweet shop (4.1) benefits it seemed the right option.

We lost contact but whenever the middle child appeared to be in crisis, I always text them to let them know that I loved them and that I was (and still am) there for them if/whenever they may need it. One time I offered to meet up for a hot chocolate, which they accepted, and slowly we started to build a new, equal relationship together.

Using my experience with our middle child as a reference point, rather than referring them to as the 'difficult' child. I would say almost imagine wrapping them in the cosiest blanket and nurturing and reassuring them to the best of your ability.

If this is proving too hard, then do get them into counselling, provide them with a space to talk about how life is for them now. We can never assume that we know, that's disrespectful and condescending – we are not them!

They say time is a healer and it is, but try as the children might to resist you or resist the new blended family, do not give up on them, do not let them slip away – they need you more than you may realise but may not be able to articulate that to you. Again remember, they are the child.

If one adult is struggling, tag each other, take it in turns. If you notice your partner is wilting, ask them what they need to bounce back. If your partner is vocal in a negative way take them to one side, give them space to offload but not where other 'ears' can hear. If not, this can have a huge detrimental effect on the relationship with the child – even if the partner feels there is no relationship so it doesn't matter – it does.

My historical memories with our middle child were very, very sad and bad. I never envisaged that my relationship with this sibling would become good. I could not have thought it possible and at times I had no idea how a good relationship would look. However, we both got older and we both learnt to communicate.

During a particularly bad time for my middle stepchild, I was there 100% through thick and thin with him. It took all my strength to be positive, reassuring and nurturing – although having been hurt myself within this relationship – I wholeheartedly needed to be the adult here.

However, they found courage and strength and belief in themselves and grew and continued to grow and today they are doing amazingly well. I am incredibly proud of their achievements.

If I look back I never see the dark times, I only see the joy when their name appears on my phone, because they are checking in to see how I am, or a text telling me that they love me, or to arrange a meet up – and that was down to me listening and listening and *listening*. It was also down to them allowing me in too.

As I was writing this book and indeed this particular chapter, the irony was that I texted the 'difficult' one to see, what he was up to and whether he fancied coming over for a pizza, as his dad was away. We now have *the* most amazing relationship, which I am truly grateful for and do you know what I'm cool about not having mushrooms on my pizza!

4. House Rules

House Rules may sound a bit draconian, they might be guidelines, procedures, expectations, manners, behaviours, etiquette, or how you and your family conduct themselves. But whatever guise they fall under, you and your family do have them.

Again, this is what used to happen before the rupture in your family, and it will continue to happen in 'the new blended family'. The difference is that these may have altered since the departing of the parent.

Ok, it's grab and a pen and piece of paper time...

Write down, what the house rules were before the change in family dynamics. I am not saying you are going to start again or that they no longer apply, but initially whilst everyone is getting (or not getting) used to the adjustment, the 'rules' may be a bit too much for your child to adhere to.

Like I just said, we are not looking at shelving them altogether but once you have your list, highlight the top three that you would really like them to abide by. If you only have three, highlight the one that you would really like them to undertake.

Once you have decided on this, it may be helpful to have a conversation with your child and explain to them that you understand the changes that you are all adapting to. Whilst taking the recent changes into consideration, you would like them to try and achieve house rule #1 (or #3). Reiterate that the other house rules will return over time, but that you do not want them to have too much to contend with during this 'settling' period.

Your child will want boundaries more than ever. They will crave these (even though they won't actually use those words or indeed act out that way), and will be seeking reassurance, that you will not be abandoning them any time soon either.

So keeping some structure is important, it just doesn't need to be quite so rigid, so that a) they may fail and b) to take the pressure off of you and hopefully make you not feel quite the dragon or evil parent, that you may have been feeling over the last few days, weeks or months during this unsettling time for you also.

Over several chapters, we will look at the impact of house rules in quite some detail. But for now, hopefully this will give you some comfort in being able to relax the constraints for the time being.

4.1. Sweet shop vs. grocery store

As I have mentioned previously, children like boundaries, they keep them safe and send them signals, that they are cared for and valued. Now even as adults, we like to feel safe, cared for and valued so recognising the positive side to boundaries is beneficial to everyone.

It may even be helpful to explain why you set boundaries and reiterate to your child, that they are there to keep them safe and to show them that they are cared for and valued.

Otherwise, children can sometimes feel that adults just do that 'because they are adults', or that the adults want to spoil their fun, or they simply don't understand what it's like to be a young person – let us not forget that we have all been that young person!

So, why am I talking about a sweet shop and a grocery store? Similar to chapter (7.4) and GPS – Guilty Parent Syndrome, a home could also be played out this way, i.e. like a sweet shop.

A sweet shop has lots of temptation, a child can feel overwhelmed in sweet shop and find it difficult to make a decision, and they may not be considering their teeth for example, in their choices for instance.

Where as in a grocery store, there are lots of different options and choices. I am sure if you were to ask most children where they might like to live, a sweet shop would probably be their preference.

The way these shops play out in blended families can be like this:

One parent (the sweet shop owner) allows the children unlimited time on their devices, has no set bed time/routine and allow the children to set their own rules irrespective of previous house rules.

The parent may do this for an easy life, to look cool, to be 'better' or more fun than the other parent, or they may be lacking in parenting techniques. The parent may treat it more like a sleepover with friends, rather than parent and child time.

The parent with the grocery store, will have boundaries, limit device time, and have a set routine at bedtime, which could of course change at weekends and school holidays. This is where the grocery store is different to the sweet shop.

For example, just because all of their friends are watching *Love Island*, it may not be age appropriate for your child to watch it, but when they are at the other parent's house aka sweet shop, they are allowed to watch it.

I do agree this can be confusing for the child and at times infuriating for them (and infuriating for the other parent too), particularly if they are unable to watch or do something that they can do at their 'other home'. This can be more difficult for the young person if the set up between the two parent's houses are week on week off.

This is not about pointing the finger at one parent, but to draw your attention to how it can be really difficult for the children to make sense of boundaries and how safe their world is.

They may question how come dad/mum allows me to do that and their other parent doesn't? They could feel that they are being punished in some way because the parents no longer like each other but it is being taken out on them. Again, it can be really helpful to have these discussions about boundaries with your child.

In my previous relationship, my then stepchild was very much living in the sweet shop at his dad's, and boy if I tried to suggest any changes. It was obviously met with a very determined and challenging young person who didn't want to change because it worked for them and their dad before me, so what's the problem?! Well the problem was, we went to bed at the same time, amongst other things.

So over time I introduced bath time before bedtime to help them unwind from the computer games. We read bedtime stories, which soon became the norm and very much looked forward to.

I worked on creating a consistent nurturing home, they drew dinosaurs at the breakfast bar, whilst I cooked dinner and we chatted easily. None of these things happened quickly and yes at times they slipped back into the old ways and were met with resistance.

I remember dropping them off once and their mum coming out to speak to me saying how different they had been since I have been on the scene. They are much calmer and they even tidied their bedroom!

In my blended family today, the children's other parental home was the BEST sweet shop in the land, they literally could do what they like and generally sounds like they did.

Yet when they came to ours, and we had our bedtime routine, or helping tidy up after dinner etc. This was at times met with challenging comments. However their dad and me would repeatedly explain that we love them and care for them and that we all need to be considered and that we all work together as a family.

Most of the time, this worked but at times you could see their furrowed brow, where they were trying to work out how the two homes could be so glaringly different. How were their two parents who at one point lived together could now having such contradicting ideas – didn't the grocery store owners realise children wanted to live in a sweet shop – all the time!

I acknowledge that not all separated parents can have amicable conversations or communication, something I feel can be so detrimental to everyone's wellbeing in the long run. But this may be what it is and if that's the case then – ok.

However if this is the case, it could be really beneficial if there is a way where one, two or three things are the same in both houses. Even if, it's on school nights only, just to make the transition for all parties concerned run that bit smoother.

As a rule we only allowed sleepovers to happen on weekends and school holidays.

In my experience, sleepovers tend to be nights that children generally don't sleep well, eat too many sugary things and then turn into an unrecognisable child the next day, which is never fun for anyone!

But, this rule would often rear its head and be argued over because the other parent allowed it, so what's the problem? This is where it can start to feel incredibly tricky not to turn this into an anti-Ex conversation/argument.

As hard as it can seem, stick to your grocery store beliefs, be consistent and communicate. Ask your child how it feels for them to not be able to have a mid-school week sleepover, or watch *Love Island*, predominantly it may come down to peer pressure and the fear of being left out or being the odd-one-out.

There will be times, when you may want to fold, because it is easier, you get a 'night off' if they sleep at a friend's, particularly if you've had a difficult week too. However, if you do it once, they will expect to be able to do it again and again.

When both parents can create a similar balanced home, it will be advantageous to everyone. Your child will be able to say to friends, that they can't do sleepovers during the school week at all, so then there is no confusion.

Otherwise, on alternative weeks where they are/aren't allowed sleepovers, your child may have to explain it was because they were at their other parent's house, which can lead to them resenting their parents who run the grocery store. It can also lead to further dislike about the breakup of their parents.

Remember to treat your home like a good meal, balanced and nutritional, so that everyone can flourish and grow positively.

5. The Old Family, Now Revised

This may seem very obvious, on the other hand, it may not. In my opinion, I am not sure how much time is given to the new dynamics and changes within the 'old family now revised'.

Yes, I am sure individually you are aware of how you are feeling about your 'absent partner', but what has actually been discussed or acknowledged? What needs to be looked at now that the person is potentially no longer part of yours and the family's everyday life?

Say for instance the person who has left used to walk the dog in the morning, last thing at night or took the dog to a dog socialising club. Who is going to do that now, or has the dog left with the other person as well – what impact does that have – positive and negative?

In our home we have pink and blue jobs, not all jobs are divided this way and of course, pink and blue jobs can be done by either of us!

However I am fairly sure that your partner, who is no longer there, would have had their role in the home. It could have been laying the breakfast things out in the morning, making a coffee first thing or putting the bins out. Again a conversation with your child could take place to understand how that might be revised.

You may feel that certain things won't be that significant and therefore won't need to be discussed, or actually it's a relief to the household in general now that that parent has left the home.

However, never assume that certain things won't need discussing. To you it may be a relief or of no interest but to your child it could mean something else.

Exercise time: If you are able to do so, sit in your home, car or coffee shop, whichever feels easier to do and then replay the person in your home.

Watch what they would have done in each room. Did they have 'their' seat in the lounge or at the dining table? Did they have 'their' cup or glass for instance? Where did their coat hang?

All of these things matter. All of these traits from that parent will have been noted and are now potentially missed.

My dad always wore literally tonnes of aftershave, to the point where you could tell what mug he drank his tea out of, even after it had been through the dishwasher! When he left, the aftershave left too and for me I felt really sad no longer being able to 'smell' my dad, because whatever took place between my mum and dad, he was still my dad and I for one, wanted his aftershave back!

I didn't consider this at the time, but I suppose I could have bought a bottle of his aftershave to smell. To be honest that may have probably not been received too well by members of the 'revised family'.

Certainly reflecting back and having an open discussion about it, may have been helpful for me and also if my mum had found a bottle of aftershave hidden in my room. Notice the word hidden there I would have felt that it couldn't have been 'on show'.

Whilst I appreciate you may not wish to look at this, but no matter you now feel about your Ex, they were and still are part of your family, in one shape or other.

5.1. What changes now mum/dad have gone?

In the early days, due to the logistics of my partner's children – one week on and one week off – there were days when I would go to my partner's house and days when I didn't.

We were in the process of building our new relationship (see 10.3) and before I was introduced to the rest of the children (my partner had his eldest child living with him full time) we needed to make sure that *we* were ok.

During this time, when we sat at the dining room table, I naturally sat side-by-side to my partner on their right side, it just happened that way.

However when I finally met the children and eventually stayed for a meal, I automatically assumed that was where I would be sitting, which I did, but at the time, it never struck me 'whose seat' could I be sitting in.

I think this only dawned on me when I was going out for an evening meal with girlfriends and noticed one of the children move from their 'regular' seat to mine.

Now I am not going to analyse what was going on, but I would really like you to reflect/be aware of this and other 'spaces' that your Ex used to fill as explained earlier.

As a stepparent, I encourage you to ask your partner where their Ex sat, or where their coat hung. You could ask what pink or blue jobs they did – remember knowledge is a good thing. The children will notice if you are doing something that their mum or dad used to do. Seeing you do that 'task', it could anger them or make them feel sad as that parent isn't there anymore.

These changes are not solely limited to blended families, as this can also be the case, when a sibling goes to university or moves out. Again, I wholly encourage this to be looked at. Sometimes we take things for granted and not fully take on board the impact of someone leaving the family home, even in a good way.

However, the children will generally be a few steps behind you in relation to a separation. It could be that the parent that no longer lives with them used to read them their bedtime story and maybe they still crave that.

I appreciate you may no longer want your Ex in your home for whatever reason, but could they read the bedtime story on set days even if it is just in the early days. If that is too difficult, could they *FaceTime* your child and read them their story that way?

Sometimes we may think we know what's best or feel the need to protect our children when making decisions. Nevertheless, children are generally pretty good at coming up with ideas around how to deal with these changes too.

Never underestimate a child's perspective or ideas, as I feel they tend to say things as they are and can be very logical, although I appreciate not all the time, they are after all a child.

Remember, you haven't got to make most decisions immediately. If you child has come up with an idea, you could say, "That's an interesting idea, let me think about that." Or you could ask your child how they feel their idea may help them, or what it is that they are scared of.

It could be that they are worried about being 'forgotten' or that their parent will be lonely. Again, you will not know their thought process unless you ask them. We are back to the C word again, *Communication*.

My dad used to sit in this big 'wing-backed' leather chair by the fire, and that was indeed *his* chair. When he was at work, we children had no qualms about sitting in that chair, particularly when the fire was lit.

However after he left, I don't remember seeing anyone sit in 'his' chair. It was as if the chair became 'un-sittable' and all that remained was 'the ghost of dad'. (Even though he was very much alive and kicking!)

Another area to consider, is that you may have a hundred and one ideas on what changes you would like to make now that your Ex has 'left the building', so again remember you are steps ahead of your child.

You may have been running through all sorts of changes or 'clearing out' ideas, but please bear in mind the impact this could have on your child. As you can see, I cannot reiterate this enough.

For your child, they may have recently been told that their parents are splitting up, and the next thing is that their 'home' is now also undergoing changes and no longer looking like their home did previously. This can be very stressful for them.

Now, I'm not saying children are like cats, but when we were moving recently, we had access to our new home before we had sold our current home. At this stage all my stepchildren had moved into their own homes. So it was just my partner and I and our two cats – simple!

During this time we started to move items from our current home, over to our new house, in order to start to create our new home.

What we didn't consider was the impact of our current home being 'stripped out'. Cardboard boxes appeared and disappeared and this affected our two cats – a lot! Both of them got incredibly stressed, because they didn't understand what was happening.

Through seeing the impact that this had on our cats *(I am pleased to say they absolutely love our new home and are completely chilled),* I feel it is prudent to be consciously aware of any changes you make and how this may impact your child.

Sometimes 'getting rid' of traces of the Ex, could be interpreted that your child is not allowed to talk about them. Or that their parent is forever erased from their home, which again could be really difficult for them.

Especially consider this, if this is your child's 'family home' where they will spend most of their time (due to the changeover arrangements). Their parent's other home will more than likely have different items and therefore both homes will fundamentally have no artefacts or home comforts that they are used to.

For children consciously and subconsciously the world can feel like an 'unsafe place' and as '*Maslow's Hierarchy of Needs*' explains, we all need a secure base.

I am not saying to have a shrine for the absent parent or that you are not allowed to change the home, but consider speaking to your child about the changes you are considering. Ask your child whether they may like something of their absent parents in their room, or together make a scrapbook /memory box of items. Instead of what may seem like 'sweeping it under the carpet', get talking about it.

Believe me, it wasn't all sadness when my dad left. It was rare that my dad was ever home from work to eat with us and the times that he did eat with us it was way too tense and strict. Thereby this change in family dynamics proved a huge relief for me at future mealtimes.

You may be surprised, that as you start to talk about making some changes, your child may ask for their room also to be changed. They may ask if they could change the shed into a den for instance. So not everything is a negative, it's just about being more aware and conscious, and, again, talking about it!

You may be keen to get new bedding and therefore you could ask if your child would like new bedding for their previous family home and take their old bedding to their new parents home, so that they have something familiar there.

As I mentioned previously, the now absent parent may have had their share of the daily household chores. For the now single parent, it would not be uncommon and unreasonable to delegate some of these chores, i.e. laying of the table, walking the dog, cooking etc., although it would be incredibly astute to involve your child in these discussions.

I understand that for some, your child may be ok with this, as they may like the idea of learning to cook. However, your child may resent the break up further as these chores could impact on their playtime. As I said, this is not unreasonable, just try not to 'drop it' on them!

I never forget a friend of mine whose dad moved his new partner in. Previously when they lived with both parents, it was really relaxed and with what appeared to be with no real set chores.

However, fast-forward to shortly after the new partner moving in. It was day one of our summer holidays and I arrived at their house only to be equally stunned with each one's written list of daily chores. Our faces were an absolute picture, which the new partner noted (and ignored) but sternly explained this was how it was going to be!

I look back now and realise the 'chores' were actually ok, but at the time they were a shock to the system, even for me although I wasn't on the receiving end.

The point I am making here is, that a) the father was nowhere to be seen, when the chores were handed out, and b) there had been no discussion, pre-warning or explanation of it.

This section can be played out both when you are separated and indeed when you enter into a blended family.

I would like you to imagine that before your partner left (or you left your partner), and as a family you always had a roast on Sunday come rain or shine. Cast your mind back and remember how Sundays felt for you. Did you look forward to the roast or did you crave something different? Did your child share their views about the roast or not? Who made the roast, or carved it?

You may be wondering what the point is, but I would ideally like you to consider as much of that 'tradition' as you can. If it helps then write it down and do give yourself space to look at this, as I am aware this can bring up emotions for you.

Now that you are separated, you may feel that you would like to continue with roasts on a Sunday, or you may feel relieved not to have them anymore, either of these thoughts are ok. However for your child, consistency in a world that has recently changed and become inconsistent may be really helpful or feel stabilising for them.

Perhaps you could talk about Sunday roasts with your child and suggest that you have them every other week, or once a month. Your child may prefer to not have them anymore but you would like them so talk about this and possibly the 'non-roast' day you could take it in turns to choose the meal for that day?

The whole point of this exercise, is whilst you may (or may not) want to eradicate your past, it can be really helpful for your child to have some things that remain constant.

Let's fast-forward and you are now entering into a blended family and your new partner always goes out for a Sunday roast. Again, talk about this together with your partner and look at how this works with your current arrangement. If we were to look at this over four weeks, one could be a roast at home, one having a roast out and the other two Sundays are non-roast days.

You may be exhausted thinking wow, it's only a roast dinner! But, for your child it may mean much more than that.

So again, I would strongly encourage you to consider changes that are being made or indeed changes that you may like to make. Remember, you are now in the process of rebuilding your child's foundation in order to make them feel safe and secure.

So, no matter how insignificant you feel something is, never assume.

6. Feelings

The word feelings, seems to have the same majority effect as when someone says "Oh there's a spider"! People seem to run for their lives or take cover. (Or is that just me?)

Why is that? What is it about looking at, considering or just the thought of you or someone being curious about your feelings that appear to make people feel vulnerable?

We all have feelings and they aren't always negative. We can have moments of joy, laughter and contentment, none of those are scary (like spiders), or whatever it is that you aren't too keen on. (You can tell spiders are not for me!)

When people look at their feelings, they tend to 'think' about them as opposed to *feel* their feelings. People go straight to their head rather than their body. I get that, it feels safer.

Another way to look at feelings is if you were to imagine a thermometer. A thermometer tells us the temperature and your feelings in a way do the same. Your feelings help you to understand when you are feeling sad, or something isn't quite sitting right, or when you feel nervous initially and then begin to feel more at ease.

Like the thermometer, when it shows hot or cold for instance you will react to that, i.e. if it's cold, you will wrap up warmer if you're going out, or if it's getting hot, you may move your phone or tablet into the shade.

Basically you react but before you react you make a conscious effort to be aware of the change in temperature. That is no different to your feelings.

So rather than run for your life, just notice how you felt when I started talking about feelings. If you can try to remember your initial reaction, as you came to this chapter and saw the word feelings, and now having read a bit about feelings, how do you *feel*?

I can't stress the importance of listening to our feelings enough. Back in the days when we were cave men and cave women our feelings, *fight, flight* and *freeze* kept us out of danger. As much as we had to listen to them to survive it is still crucial to listen to them now, as these form our gut feelings.

I feel the need to reassure you that nothing bad is going to happen, if you acknowledge your feelings. Ok, so maybe you are feeling something that you'd rather not or other people won't approve of – but that's ok!

An example of this could be you're at a party and everyone seems to be enjoying themselves. However, you would ideally like to go home, as that is how you feel and how you choose to react to your feelings is entirely up to you.

You may leave the party and that's where you may feel other people may disapprove or you may stay and just accept you are thinking about other people's feelings. I am not saying which is right and which is wrong but the most important bit, is that you are noticing *your* feelings and therefore noticing *you*! – This is a great start!

6.1. But this is how I feel!! – Couldn't you have tried harder to make it work?

Sometimes it can be really hard to acknowledge, accept or understand how someone feels when it conflicts with what we are feeling.

The situation could be that you or someone you know is in the process of separating, or have separated and are now divorcing. You may be a parent, a child, a family member or a friend entwined in one of the above processes and because you are entwined in some way, it will have an effect on you – and you will feel different, because we are all unique.

You may prefer the term impact, but either way, your feelings will be reacting to what is going on, which is totally understandable.

This is about giving yourself the space to acknowledge how you feel – I mean how you *really* feel, uncensored and true to you. *Or* allowing your child to say how they really feel uncensored and true to them.

So what do I mean by being uncensored, and how do we do this? Sometimes when we may be feeling a certain way, we can talk ourselves out of it or brush it off.

For example, we can tell ourselves we are being stupid to think like that, or what would X think if they knew that's how I felt? You may even say to yourself that your friends would tell you to get tougher. We can become really good at talking ourselves out of how we are feeling or dismissing our feelings altogether.

It never ceases to amaze me how many clients I witness literally swallowing down their feelings. This could be due to shame, embarrassment, or a manner of other reasons.

One of the things that strikes me the most is, when clients are 'pleased' to not have cried in a session. I get that, as I felt the same at times when I saw my counsellor, I'd think, 'Can I not attend one session without crying – jeeez!'

However I am acutely aware there were times when I didn't cry and knew it was because I started to feel more comfortable with what we were looking at. There were also times when I 'resisted giving into the tears' because I so badly didn't want to feel sad or upset about whatever was affecting me. So I do honestly get it.

Allow me to share the power of embracing your feelings…

You will actually feel less stressed, you will make decisions that will be more helpful to you as opposed to hinder or cause you more stress, tiring etc., etc. Giving yourself the space to cry and acknowledge why you feel tearful is saying, "I hear you body, and I accept that's how I feel right now." (This isn't how you are going to feel forever.)

Clients who look mortified of the thought of 'giving in' to their tears, I often encourage them to cry in the shower. Your eyes don't get puffy, no one can tell you've been crying if that's an issue for you and you probably won't be heard either.

Another possibility could be to watch a sad film. When I sit and watch *Pretty Woman* (my go-to film), no one will be any the wiser that the tears aren't about Julia Roberts and Richard Gere, they may just wonder why I'm not watching something a bit more cheery!

If someone is uncomfortable with you crying, that will be their stuff and they can sit with being uncomfortable as opposed to you not allowing your tears to run freely. Another fear, could be that that you are worrying that the tears might never stop – trust me – they will.

The same applies to your child. Giving them the tools to share and express how they feel could also be really positive for them. Allowing them to be honest with themselves how they are feeling about the separation/divorce.

It may be too raw or difficult for you to hear how they are feeling, or you may find yourself questioning 'was it really that bad', or 'how can I/am I doing this to my child?'.

If that is the case, think about if there is another member of the family or a good friend or teacher, who you feel your child may be able to talk to, or indeed a counsellor. They may even have a counselling facility at your child's school/college/university.

As I said in the introduction, I don't remember my parents being quite at breaking point, or maybe I did and just shoved my teenager head in the sand a bit further? But I do remember how I felt.

I remember I had a friend over the day my dad came back to collect some of his belongings. I just stayed 'frozen' in my room not knowing what to do, feeling incredibly uncomfortable and awkward because my friend was there.

I also felt really sad for my dad. The fact that he came into the house, our family home and none of his children spoke to him or tried to stop him. I desperately wanted to run to him and hug him, but I knew the tears would fall and I didn't want my friend to see the pain that would have been etched on my face, so I just froze until he left.

Did I ever tell anyone about that? I talked a lot about my parents' divorce when I was in counselling. Together my counsellor and I undid the years of knots that were created as a result of suppressing my feelings. But no, you are the first to read about it and so it just goes to show how 'clever' we are at burying difficult issues in order to 'be ok'.

The only setback about suppressing our feelings is that eventually they will rise to the surface. Sometimes our body decides that we no longer need to be carrying these unappreciated feelings.

So, with that in mind, I truly recommend space to be provided for you and your child to look at the good, the bad and the ugly/vulnerable feelings. No one needs to make sense of them, it's amazing how powerful it can be just to give them space and acknowledge them.

So if your child says, "Couldn't you have tried harder?" ask them how they are feeling or what is going on for them to say that or indeed what do they mean by that? Again, this may not be face to face, it could be whilst they are playing with their *Lego*, drawing, or on their device, if that's the case draw with them or play *Lego* with them. This will feel safer for your child and could be helpful for you to have a distraction too.

The plus side of doing something like drawing together, is that you haven't got to look at each other as both of your eyes can be focused on what it is that you are actually doing.

On the flip side, if your child isn't saying anything, do not presume that everything's ok. If they are being quiet or noncommunicative do not automatically put it down to being a 'moody teenager' (a phrase that really pushes my buttons!).

This is so important and key; be really aware if your teenager is spending a significant amount of time in their room or just saying they are 'fine'. Yes, you may have asked your friend their opinion and they may say their teenager is the same, however, it is not wise to put all teenagers in the same category.

Your teenager, may really be missing their other parent, or may have school issues, but with 'everything' else going on, they may not want to trouble you or be a pain. Or on the other hand, they may feel it is a taboo subject.

I remember a colleague once saying about watching people in a swimming pool, "It's not the ones making all the noise that you need to worry about but the quiet ones will probably need your attention more."

Hmmm, but that's not to say that the 'loud' child needs ignoring, quite the opposite. It just means they are communicating in a very different way.

Sometimes we can assume that our children are 'dealing with it really well'. I am curious about that comment. What does 'dealing with it really well' look like; shouting and crying or being super helpful and no trouble at all for example?

Remember we are all as unique as our fingerprints and the same goes for how we deal with emotions too.

6.2.   You think it's tough?!

I appreciate separation, divorce and then potentially blended families may have been or still is tough for you.

I will continue to repeat that you need to find the right outlets for you to discuss and share how difficult it has been or still is for you. Ideally this will be with other adults that will support you, whatever that support looks like.

This could be a 'fixer' – someone who likes to solve problems, someone who will sit with your discomfort or someone who can provide you with some much-needed respite and distraction!

However, we are going to look at how it may be seen through the eyes of your child.

When I talk about 'it' being tough, I could be referring to anything that has happened when the 'nuclear' family has separated or, perhaps there has only ever been one parent in their life and now there is another adult. It could be managing the impact of an estranged parent, or getting used to new family arrangements with 'add-ons'.

Remember, for your child, they can't simply say, "This isn't working for me so let's end this relationship" or, in most cases the option to move out is not obtainable. Instead they are faced with these new changes and for want of a better expression, they may pretty much feel like they have to 'like it or lump it'!

If it has always been the two of you or the only child in the family, suddenly when those dimensions change, life may feel unstable or cause conflict when your time is now being divided between your child and a new partner in your life. Adding to the challenge your partner's child that could also have been thrown into the mix.

I am not for one moment saying that you asked to be in this situation, but your child most probably didn't either. So when you feel they are acting up or being disruptive, try and get on their level and find out what is going on for them, and what they are finding challenging at that moment in time.

You may find yourself feeling that you know the reason why they are being quiet or disruptive, not engaging, or lethargic. Because they are your child and you know them *right…* Wrong!

Children can be incredibly good at not being a burden, not causing their parents any or further distress. They may choose to not upset their parents or disappoint them in any way but instead battle on with the many varying daily 'demons' that they may struggle with.

You may have a child who has gone to university or is working full time, that doesn't mean they don't have their own anxieties. Children and young people can be incredibly creative in disguising what is going on for them.

It never ceases to amaze me the amount of young people I see in my practice who struggle with making phone calls, sending emails and general day-to-day tasks. Something you may take for granted. Yet have no idea your child is finding one or all of those hard.

In a world where 'change is good' and we are deemed as

change advocates, change can be very scary and daunting.

I was reminiscing the other day when my family and I used to visit my Nan and granddad, and how wonderful it was. What was really wonderful was that nothing had changed, because they and their home was consistent. This in turn provided a safe space, where I always felt comfortable and held.

So imagine what happens when the rug is literally ripped from underneath your child's feet; the world can feel uncomfortable and definitely not safe.

Fear not, all is not lost, there are some simple measures that you can put in place to help provide security and reassurance.

Exercise time: Firstly, if you have the opportunity try placing yourself in their shoes, literally sit or stand at their level and try seeing their world/home that might be changing through their eyes.

Really look at things in detail, spend time doing this. Imagine home (including new family members), school, friendship groups, clubs and activities, what impact could these changes have on your child?

I am not expecting or even suggesting for you to change your decision, as I am sure that you would have thought about whatever the change was and the ramifications of said change. All I am asking you to do, is to swap your view to your child's *potential* point of view.

I would like us to now look at a situation whereby you now have a new partner and they also have a child.

You are at a stage where you would like to tell your child about this new partner. You may have been playing conversations over in your head and for fear of how your child may react, you may be trying (what you may feel) to put a positive spin on this new news for your child.

It may look like "I have met someone and they have a child too who is also your age so that's great isn't it?!" Or, "You will now have someone to play with." They may well see it like you hope, then again maybe not.

My dad's new partner had a child around my age. I was grateful that they didn't attend the same school, but imagine my shock when a friend at school approached me and started asking about my dad in his new relationship, as they knew the other child!

I felt incredibly ashamed and yes, another part of my world was 'tainted' by my parent's separation. I had chosen not to tell anyone (apart from my best friend) what was happening, as parents' divorcing was less common in those days. My reason for this was simply that I didn't want to be looked upon as being different and I definitely didn't want to be 'talked about' either, especially not be the subject of school gossip!

This is no different to the introduction and the train ride previously mentioned. Your child is still playing catch-up, and as you may be super happy or not, they may be super happy or not too.

I have indeed worked with several children and young people, who are in fact relieved that their parents are no longer together. For them it feels much easier not living under the same roof as both of them. Children and young people have also shared their joy at having another 'mum' or feel their stepdad gets them more than their dad, so, it's not all doom and gloom!

Again, notice what your child is saying, how they are saying it, when they are saying it and also notice what your child may not be saying or doing something as well. They will give you clues even if they are subtle and even if you are choosing not to see them.

The sooner you open up good communication methods (8.1) the sooner feelings will start to be heard and considered.

I cannot stress the importance of feelings and how we can dismiss them or refuse to acknowledge them. This could be because it is too painful or for fear of the impact of saying how you feel. However once feelings start to be discussed and noticed, you and your child will start to 'feel' their place in the new family or relationship and know that they matter and are considered and seen.

It is really important to not put it down to them being a

'moody teenager' or whatever labels you may give them, even if your friend confirms that their teenager is acting the same. Your teenager and their teenager are two entirely different people and need to be treated as such.

I feel like I have lectured in this chapter and I apologise, if that is how it has come across. I wouldn't blame you if you felt a bit perturbed about why it seems to be all about your child.

What about you and how you feel? Of course I am considering you, which is why by noticing your children's feelings, hopefully you will start to acknowledge yours and listen to your needs too.

6.3. The estranged parent

This is quite an interesting area. If you were to think of the estranged parent what thoughts come immediately to mind? What are your immediate feelings about the estranged parent?

Whether you are the parent or stepparent to the estranged parent, you will both almost probably have completely different thoughts and feelings about this. Both are actually ok.

In chapter (7.2) where I talk about keeping certain conversations for 'adult ears only', this is also included in that capacity too. As the adult (parent), I appreciate how hard it is to literally bite your tongue, when you may want to say out loud, what you think of them. Particularly if something occurred in that moment in time.

This however will not be helpful to your child. Again, what could happen is that the estranged parent becomes 'unspoken', almost as if they didn't exist! Although I appreciate in some situations you may have wished, that they hadn't ever existed.

But if we go back to the 'unspoken parent', this can cause great conflict for your child. They may want to talk about their parent they may be struggling with unanswered questions about why or how their other parent has become estranged. Whilst you may not be able to answer their questions, it could be really helpful and important for your child to know that it is ok to talk about the 'absent' parent.

Another area which I feel is also really important to acknowledge, is that the missing parent never, metaphorically speaking ever goes away. They 'appear' on your child's birthday, Mother's Day or Father's Day or at Christmas for example.

For someone who is not physically present is actually present an awful lot of the time. The missing parent could 'materialise' at a school play, or when their best friend talks about the same sex parent, whom theirs is 'absent'.

I am all too aware how people can curse having to accommodate their parents, say at Christmas, and I am also aware how many people would be overjoyed to have one more Christmas with their parent(s).

As previously mentioned, you as the parent are not expected to have all the answers, but what your child may find helpful, is to have their own 'parent' journal. This journal can be where they can write questions to them or write to them about how their day has been.

In having a 'parent journal', I feel this can be really important for your child as this keeps a line of communication going, albeit one way. What this provides, is that it gives your child permission to acknowledge their estranged parent. The journal can be in written form and/or drawn in – there are no rules for the journal.

The estranged parent will be impacting on them and the journal will enable you to recognise that whilst they are not playing a tangible part in your child's life, they are definitely still part of their life.

This could also be beneficial if your child has negative thoughts towards the estranged parent. The journal can act as a channel to write down and recognise how these feelings may be impacting on your child's life currently, and indeed what they could take through to their adult years, which will possibly not be healthy.

If you decide to explore the option of a parent journal with your child, do ask them if they would like to share what they write in it or indeed let them know that you are ok with them sharing their contents with you, even if you might struggle with what they have written/drawn. What you will be communicating to your child is that I respect this is important to you and not silly or pointless.

Another part of understanding the impact that the estranged parent has had on your child, could be for you to ask them if they have any questions that they would have liked to have asked their parent. Or if they were to meet up with them, what would they hope it could be like?

This exploration can also help initially for you, to see how they have 'pigeonholed' the estranged parent. Your child may have romanticised the situation, so that they have imagined, when they meet up, the parent will 'save' or 'rescue' them, they will be their 'knight in shining armour'.

I am going to use the term 'play'. I would like you and your child to 'play' with their ideas of, what they feel might happen or indeed believe it actually will.

You will no doubt have your own view on what is likely to happen, but the important part about playing is exactly that, *to play*. When we play, we can be creative and imagine all sorts of things, we are not bound by reality or structure.

Although, I do appreciate this exercise could create feelings, thoughts or reactions for you, which certainly doesn't feel like fun! Again, that's ok just ensure you share these with an adult and not your child.

So what does 'play' look like? Well, depending on the age of your child it could be having the conversation, when they are literally playing with their toys say *Lego* for instance.

Your child will already be in 'play and imaginative mode', so if they were to start talking about their parent, you could ask where would they could feature if they were playing with your *Lego*, or which *Lego* person is mummy or daddy.

I am not expecting you to be a counsellor here, but what you are allowing is to open up communication and this is the first part.

For another child it could be asking them 'if you could sit on a magic carpet with your (estranged) mum or dad where could it take you, what would you choose for you both to do?"

This new information that you may have uncovered may never be needed. However, if we were to go back to the romanticised version, it will provide you with the knowledge, of your child's romanticised view.

Imagine that the estranged parent did get in contact with you and asked to meet up with your child. You could use this opportunity to advise the estranged parent of the potential expectation of your child.

If, on the other hand, you are almost 100% sure that the estranged parent will not be able to meet your child's expectations, hold this in mind. Ideally at some point, you may be able to talk to your child and tentatively explain how their expectations will possibly not be met.

I remembered as a young teenager and again later in my adult years what my 'reunion' would be like when I saw my dad. A huge amount of estranged years had passed and I had imagined him to be my knight in shining armour. (*I was after all 'daddy's girl'.*) He was automatically going to apologise for all his 'wrongdoings' (in my 15-year-old young person's eyes) and make everything better.

However the reality was, he was always going to be himself. He was completely unaware of my expectations and thoughts of what I felt were his 'wrongdoings'. In actual fact, we never spoke about what happened or more to the point what didn't happen, and how I ended up with this fantasy of him rescuing his 'little girl'! (Fear not, having been in counselling myself, I've worked through this.)

How I describe my feelings, I kept them firmly to myself. Importantly for me, no one knew this was how I felt. My dad was very much a taboo subject at home and through no one's fault, it was never deemed 'a thing' for me to talk to someone. Adults probably saw me as 'being fine'.

Having been in counselling and completed my degree in counselling, I do feel that I would have benefited if I had been able to talk openly about my feelings and thoughts, regarding my dad when I was younger.

I also acknowledge, that as a 15-year-old I may have said I was 'fine' and didn't need to speak to anyone. Looking back, I would have liked to have been strongly encouraged to attend several sessions, in order for me to recognise it was a safe place to say how I was feeling.

A child with an estranged parent is a loss, it is an ending without an end. Unlike when someone dies, an estranged parent lives on but not within your child's life. Again, for all you avid counsellors and your views on this, I have done a lot of work with my dad's relationship, and mine but I would like to share this with you;

Obviously my dad is not getting any younger (nor am I). I am acutely aware, that I possibly won't see him again in person and so it is important to be aware of the 'not knowing'. For me, the 'not knowing" was what it may feel like when he dies, and that I wasn't part of his life for such a long time.

We are still estranged and have a loose relationship using email only. However, 'knowing' that our relationship works using email, for both of us, is good enough.

The most poignant thoughts are never to assume that you know how your child feels about their estranged parent, or indeed how they may feel about them throughout their life. I strongly encourage you to give them space to have the unspoken, spoken.

6.4.   Piggy in the middle

As I have previously highlighted and continue to highlight throughout the book, blended families can and do bring many challenges. They also bring some very treasured moments too!

This particular section is about, how the biological parent can feel torn; torn between their love and wants for their child, their love and wants for their new partner and indeed their love and wants for themselves.

Here, we will look at the struggles, demands, expectations

and decision-making that go along with this unique role. When I was writing this particular part, it took me back to when having previously heard people refer to themselves, as "I'm just a mother."

However when we have scrutinised this role, together we can come up with many different roles incorporated in being a mother. Here are just a few: cook, cleaner, accountant, taxi driver, 'counsellor' and referee.

As you can see, being 'a mother' is a multifaceted role!

The reason that I wanted to look at that role is because being a biological parent in a blended family also has many roles too. One too often could be 'piggy in the middle'.

What does it feel like to be 'piggy in the middle'? Well, there is more than likely a sense of feeling the need to be 'neutral' between these two parts of your family – who both equally mean the world to you.

I do recognise how your 'neutral-ability' can be tested at times, and probably on more than one occasion – to the limit!

In all of the mix of the children, your new partner and being a parent, there is *you* and your feelings, your emotions and your needs. There will be times, when it can feel pretty tricky to work out, when you can bring *these* to the forefront. This will especially be, when you are feeling like a constant fire fighter or too tired to be able to look at your needs let alone discuss them.

Exercise time: What I feel, that could be really helpful, is to write down what situations turn you into a firefighter. You could draw two columns, one for the children and one for your partner. There could even be one for your Ex!

In the first instance, I would encourage you to really pour it all out, every last ounce! Imagine you are squeezing the last bit of mayo to go with your chips (because this is the last drop in the house!). We want you to get everything out. By getting everything out means nothing can go unnoticed, about how you feel. Because this chapter is about *you*!

Because you are *important* too!

Then, I would like you to 'rate' the situations that you

have highlighted. This can be 1–10 or traffic lights, red, amber and green. Green could represent 'quick-wins' and red could represent situations that may take a bit more thought-process and navigation.

Now you have your lists, add to them your feelings. How these situations make you feel. The next part is for you to write down 'part-solutions', that you could present to each party. I acknowledge at this point, speaking to your Ex may not be an option, but we will come to this list too.

You may even be surprised, that some of the part-solutions may not need your partner or your child to adapt, but it could in fact be you that needs to adapt.

For instance, you could remove yourself away from that particular situation. There may be times where you feel the need to 'jump in' and 'rescue' one of the party. However, it may be helpful for them to learn how to deal with those difficult moments together, even though it may feel incredibly uncomfortable for you, or you feel that is your role.

What you may find helpful, is speaking to a friend about what you have written down. They may be able to offer constructive advice or a suggestion, which will come from their perspective and therefore will hopefully be emotionally neutral.

Allow yourself some time and then go back to your notes and see, if you want to make any changes or indeed add anything else that may have happened in the meantime.

Now, we are going to work on you communicating this. I do acknowledge this may sound simple and even too easy, however as I continue to say – communication is key.

Make a date with your partner, ideally on mutual territory. You may go for a walk, or go to the pub for example. Whilst I elaborate on many other ways to communicate (8.1) face to face could be really helpful here, as we need your partner, to actually *see* how hard this is for you.

Reassure your partner how you feel them about them and your relationship with them and that, you that do want to be with them. (I am assuming here that you do, otherwise there really is no need to do this!)

Now explain to them that you recognise the many challenges a blended family brings. You are sure they will have their concerns or thoughts, but for now if they are able to do so, ask them to park their feelings/thoughts.

Share with them how the dynamics in the family can cause you to feel torn, and you are concerned on how this impacts your relationship as a couple. Explain that you have identified the three areas. Then, show them your list of challenges and how each challenge makes you feel.

It may be helpful at this point to acknowledge to your partner that they may not have realised how you have been feeling or indeed how individual challenges have caused you great upset. This is ok, they are not a mind reader. You can reiterate to them that you are not expecting immediate changes, but make them aware of what is and has been going on for you.

Hopefully, you have identified at least one 'green quick-win' situation in your partner's column. So this could be the one to start with.

I feel what can be really important here is to say to your partner that you are speaking to them about this, because, a) they are an adult (as your partner may feel defensive and return to being a child – metaphorically) and b) because you want to do this together. As being a referee can feel isolating and lonely at times.

You can share what part-solutions you have come up with. Explain to them that you are not expecting them to make any decisions immediately, and that they may need time to process what you have said.

Your partner may even want time to consider some alternative part-solutions. It may even be that your partner didn't fully recognise the distress that particular situation was causing you or appreciate that they could change their reaction/ behaviour going forward.

I do feel it could be helpful to say that you have also drawn up a list for the children, and the list is something you would like you and your partner to look at together at some point. However for now, it's about you and your partner working towards 'singing from the same hymn sheet'.

Your partner may want to see your 'child's' list. I would strongly advise to not show this, as we do not want to 'dilute' it or provide a 'diversion' as to what needs to be addressed within the 'adults' first.

What can also arise from what may feel like a 'tug-of-war' relationship between your child and partner can be fear. You may be fearful, that you are unable to withstand the referee position that this 'triangular' relationship holds you in. In this instance, I cannot stress enough that you need to talk/communicate what it feels like to be a referee.

Another knock-on fear is feeling whether you will be able to sustain a relationship, as you are trying to work out and strike a balance between being a parent and having a relationship too.

In regards to the Ex's list, you could also mention this to your partner. Ideally this could be after some of the points have been addressed on your parents' and child's list.

One of the pressing points could be how you feel when you collect or drop off your child at your Ex's home. Your partner may not realise what you need, so communicate this, even if it is that you just need a glass of wine, a hug or time to talk when you return home.

7. Take Responsibility

I appreciate this section may feel similar to the feelings chapter. Imagine the feelings chapter as beginners and 'taking responsibility' is advanced.

Let me explain about taking responsibility in more detail...

Since you started the feelings chapter, you are now more aware of how you feel and potentially, what triggers cause you to feel like that. This chapter is about you *managing* your thoughts and feelings and taking ownership of them.

So, taking responsibility is exactly that, owning up to yourself about how you are feeling.

Let me give you an example of when we don't take responsibility;

Imagine one of those days when you have had a bad day at work. When you walk through the door, you may not acknowledge or realise that you are in a bad mood, however the first person that you come into contact with gets the barrage of emotion! The person on the receiving end probably looks confused as they try to quickly work out, what it is that they have done wrong.

Well behind the 'barrage of emotion' is you and your feelings.

The 'thing' that happened today (that may have been avoided) has wound you up and niggled at you throughout the day. You may have been berating yourself over whether you could have done something different or better.

So when you walked through the door and, for example, your child left their dirty cups and plates on the coffee table – THAT was an opportunity (subconsciously) to vent your frustration that has built up over the day.

What you could have done was acknowledge to yourself that you are not in a great mood. Then, knowing that it is not uncommon for your child to leave their dirty plates or cups out, which could antagonise your mood further, you could text your child before you get home. You could ask them to ensure the lounge is tidy and free of their dirty cups and plates.

In doing this you enable everyone to be on a level playing field.

In going through the above process, firstly, you have already acknowledged to yourself that you are not that chirpy. Secondly, you have also recognised what might tip your emotions out, and thirdly, your child is now also *aware* of what your expectations are. Although you have made them aware, they still may not have tidied to your standards.

This is still a really good start. Ideally through reading this book, you will become more comfortable communicating your needs.

The main difference is that if something is causing you angst with your Ex, this is where you 'take responsibility'. You refrain from sharing it with your child or taking it out on them. You continue to hold onto your feelings rather than what can feel like you passing your negative emotions onto them.

Instead, manage it in an adult way, be it talking it through with other adults, doing your exercise class or whatever else, that will help you to get these unhelpful emotions out.

Look at it like your kitchen waste bin that needs emptying, probably more times than you care to think. We need you to empty your rubbish that you are carrying to. Your rubbish needs to go in the household waste bin and not the recycled one. This rubbish is not a recyclable product for anyone.

7.1. Own it!

No matter how challenging your relationship is never and I repeat NEVER tell your child it's their fault! Yes I agree, they can be challenging, but YOU need to accept responsibility for what is <u>not</u> going well.

When parents break up, it astounds me how many young people feel that it was somehow their fault, they could have been quieter, more academic, or picked the towels off of their bedroom floor.

Children are not always privy to the downfall of their parents' relationship. Or, they are not privy to all of the downfalls of *both* parties in their parents' relationship.

A key example of this was when I once spoke to a child. They said, "I realise that if my parents (biological and stepparent) split up, it's my fault." When I questioned them how could it be their fault, it was because their parent had told them so! Anyhow, now is not the platform to go into the exact details about that scenario, BUT this is classic of when a parent shirks responsibility as the adult.

This is where both your filter and taking ownership needs to come to the forefront – this is where *you* as an adult need to take control and – own it!

I am not saying that biological parents don't have arguments about their own biological children, but I don't think either one would throw the towel in because it isn't going right with the children (although I'm fairly certain you may be able to change my viewpoint on that). I would like to think and hope, the parents would work together and include the young person in the discussions and, if necessary, get outside help in whatever form.

Don't get me wrong, I remember a time one Christmas when I was sitting on the floor of the bathroom crying, thinking I don't know how much more I can take of this. The door was locked and my youngest stepchild was standing the other side of the door and was saying, "Please don't leave." At no point, did I say "It's you kids that are making me feel like this."

Another time, in a previous relationship, I became distant from my stepchild. I am not proud to say that I became resentful. Resentful for the way his dad sprung into 'super dad' mode on the weekend that we had him, yet the other 12 days were the total opposite. (I'm not proud of how I felt and I have done a lot of work on myself since becoming a counsellor, which has enriched my life in so many ways.)

I did try to explain how I felt to my partner, I even went to relationship counselling (on my own, as they didn't want to go and didn't really see the point), but I tried, I tried so hard to make it work. But as the wonderful saying goes, you can put glitter on a poo, but it's still a poo!

I am saddened how the relationship between my previous stepchild and myself dissolved, although I still have a lot of happy memories.

I often wonder about the impact of me moving out of that household. We didn't get to say goodbye and that has often played on my mind. I hope that they never thought for one moment it was their fault that their dad and I went our separate ways. I am hoping their dad owned it and said it was because of the two of us and reassured them, that they did nothing wrong.

Relationships are tough – period! Throw in stepchildren and their other family members and it can get quite tricky to put it mildly.

Yes, you may get frustrated with sharing 'arrangements', as you may feel you never get the place to yourself.

But would you 'get the place to yourself' if you and your partner had stayed together? The answer is no. The same applies to weekends or weeks off, as 'sharing' wouldn't have been an option either.

However you are feeling, it's *you* that are feeling like that.

At this point, I need you to ask yourself, "What am I not doing for *me* in my life, that I could be doing for me?"

You may need to re-read that sentence a few times for it to make sense. But fundamentally, what it is saying, is what is it that you need, that you can provide for yourself and not, refer this irritation onto blaming for instance having your child or stepchild in your home?

We can easily blame it on the fact, that we have no 'our time'. Ask yourself what that looks like. Did you previously have your own time and if so, what did you do or not do? Again, you need to vocalise this to your partner in an adult way. Or if you are now a single parent, what could your revised own time look like now and how could it be adapted to your current parenting obligations?

The 'perk of being divorced' has got to be for me one of the most thought-provoking comments that I have heard when relating to divorce. In actual fact, I don't believe I've ever heard the word perk used in that context prior to then, and indeed since!

So what came as even more of a surprise was when a client quoted that from a stepparent. This was relating to dividing the children between the two families and manoeuvring the children in such a way that the two adults in one relationship 'get a break' from having any children in their home on a regular basis.

One of the important things as a counsellor during a client session is noticing what is going on inside myself when clients are sharing their difficulties.

In this particular session, I have to say anger pretty much erupted in me when I heard this. This was partly because of knowing where my client was mentally at that time. I would have really liked to have contacted the parents (step and biological) and invite them to have some counselling.

Understandably I didn't contact the parents, however chapter (16) (*Counselling for parents*) can highlight how you as a parent could use counselling to explore what's your stuff, and what might be your child's.

The point that I would like to make here is this. If you were to put yourself in your child's shoes and had an adult say to you, "It is a perk not having you here," how would that make you feel? I get you may really want time out, its challenging, exhausting, relentless and whatever else you may add, but *really*, a perk?!

A child should believe that their parents wanted them, chose to have them or, if they came as a surprise, welcomed them into the world and began to love them unconditionally.

I'm aware that I bleat on about communication but the other key thing here is to remember your child didn't have a choice in the matter when their parents decided to go their separate ways. Your foundation may have been rocked and theirs has been too.

This may be the first time that the world to them may feel less safe or a feeling of vulnerability. That doesn't necessarily go when their parent(s) find another partner. Your child has already encountered a rupture and, like it or not, their survival instinct will be very close to the surface. They may not have been prepared the first time, but they sure as eggs are eggs will try and be as ready as they can be for any potential ruptures in the future.

So whatever your thoughts are about dividing time as per chapter (3) keep your thoughts to yourself and between you and your partner. As I have mentioned several times, remember, no matter what their ages are, your child is *still* the child in the relationship, and you are the adult.

If you need a conversation about how long your new partner's child spends at your home or whatever it is that seems to be grating on you, please, please, *please* discuss this with your partner.

Yes, it may cause an argument, yes, you may think your partner won't want to hear what you have to say. Or understandably defend their child's situation, but it is imperative that the two adults discuss this and that your child never receives such a blow as my young client did – this is not only unkind but is totally unacceptable!

7.2. Use your filter

As I have mentioned previously, adults are adults and children are children. No matter what age the children are, whether they are 10, 18, 25 or older – if you are the 'parent' they are *still* the children.

The impact on children when you do not use your filter is very detrimental to their wellbeing. I appreciate at times that their behaviours and actions may feel detrimental to you too. The difference here is that you are the adult and parent or stepparent – it is your responsibility to be aware of what you are saying and who could potentially hear it.

Yes, even if you would like them to hear how you are feeling at that moment – you still need to use your filter and probably at that time, even more so!

So, what do I mean by filter?

Let's say for instance you are in a clothes' shop or standing in the queue of your local supermarket. As you see someone try something on, you may think 'Oh no that looks awful' or someone's food items make you think 'You shouldn't be eating that'.

Now I am not questioning why you are making those judgements, but imagine your filter stops working and you say those comments out loud. So, both of those people did hear you, and also noticed your grimacing face. How might you feel? Embarrassed or mortified, or self-righteous as you see it as helping them out?

That is why we have a filter. I am not saying whether it is right or wrong to have those judgements or feelings. Fact of the matter is that you have them and they are *yours* and that is ok. The filter will stop your feelings and thoughts from potentially hurting others.

It is even more important to have the filter on at home. I am not saying if your child is wearing something that maybe doesn't look great that you wouldn't say anything. Instead you would use your filter to prevent you from saying something that could hurt their feelings and yet still getting your view across. You could temper your comment to be more palatable and heard in a kind manner.

Let me give you an example; a stepparent and their partner were discussing grandchildren. They didn't have any yet and it was going to be a while until they did, due to the ages of their respective children. The stepparent said, "Well obviously I will like my blood related/biological grandchildren more than your grandchildren."

I do not know if they knew that their partner's child was in earshot, they definitely knew that they were in the house. So, wow, can you even begin to imagine how the child that overheard that felt? Or how their thoughts about themselves were?

I can tell you now, they felt really, *really* hurt, particularly because they actually loved their stepparent and saw them as another mum/dad without the 'step'. To say they were knocked for six was an understatement.

I have no idea how the parent receiving that comment felt, or why the stepparent said what they said, but it could have been really helpful to have those types of conversations when they knew that nobody was there to witness or overhear them.

I was clearly not there, when the comment was made, and have no idea what the context was, however, I did witness the impact that it had on the young person.

Again, I am not pointing the finger at the adults, conversations take place and that's ok, of course it is, I am just asking for you to be more aware of your surroundings.

If you allow yourself to 'check-in' with how you are feeling and what is being provoked in you that could be useful. Maybe you are hurting because of something your partner has said and done or not said or not done and that was your way of hurting them (and potentially their child too?).

Let us look at this scenario; one child, biological or step is playing up, or their behaviour has always been challenging. You sense that they make the atmosphere in the house feel incredibly uncomfortable for you and the rest of the family too. Even though you may feel you want to say out loud so that they can hear, 'Why don't they go and live with the other parent, they clearly don't want to be here' – stop and breathe!

Instead, read or re-read the communications chapter (8) and work out how to communicate with the child that is exhibiting these behaviours and find out what *they* need.

The child behaving in this way may not know what they need or be able to communicate this, because they are trying to make sense of the situation. Break it down for them into bite-size pieces, i.e., changeover, school, other parents house, stepparent(s), siblings, peer pressure, *social media*... the list is endless.

If they continue to find it hard to verbalise what it is, try asking them what they don't like or what they do like. Ask them what they may need from you or other members of the family at this moment in time. It may be helpful to go for a drive or a walk when having this conversation rather than face-to-face, which can feel overwhelming or uncomfortable. You could text them, even though they are in another room, again this may feel less confrontational for the child.

Your filter needs to collect everything. This could be details of the divorce, or what the Ex *appears* to be demanding. Keeping the filter in mind, this also relates to any paperwork or phone conversations.

In the process of separation and divorce, your children do not need to know the ins and outs of what went on and what is going on. Yes, they may ask, but that doesn't mean it is necessarily healthy for them to know.

You may say to them that mum and dad are finding it tricky to talk or communicate at the moment. They don't need to know, how difficult the other parent is being, or what they are doing to make it tricky.

I get that at times, you may find yourself wanting to vent to them, what their mum or dad has just done. However, who will benefit from that information sharing? Be aware of your feelings about the situation, and notice where you are voicing them.

You may find it really helpful to have a list of friends or your own *WhatsApp* group, which you can use as an outlet for your frustrations. Or you have a word that you text your friends which means 'I need one of you right now to call me' (or ASAP).

What can happen is when one parent leaves, a child can take on the role of being another adult in the house see (7.3). I cannot stress enough how important it is, for you to be the parent/adult and for your child to remain as the child.

If a child takes on the other parental role, you (the parent/ adult) will start to share adult information with them. The child who is already caught in the middle of the separation then becomes more entrenched in your relationship with your Ex. Your child may then start to have conflict within themselves when they see the other parent and also with any siblings.

A helpful reminder is that the *Samaritans* are available 24/7, so if you would like to sound off to someone, even in the middle of the night, they will be available and it's free!

In the meantime, if you can hold in your mind that a filter is to remove contaminants – so remember to refrain from sharing everything you think – certain thoughts and comments are for adult ears or no ears only!

Another option, is to write down everything uncensored about how you are feeling and then either delete the document or print it out and shred it. As I have mentioned previously, it is important to honour and acknowledge how you are feeling, just how or who you do it with must also be considered too.

7.3.   A child becomes a role figure/adult

This so easily happens, yet I would strongly encourage you to recognise if this is happening or has happened.

If it has happened, that's ok, you can slowly undo the role figure which your child has taken on, and allow your child to return back to exactly that, a child.

When a child becomes the role figure, it can be conscious and subconscious. The conscious way could be that you say to your son, "You are now the man of the house" or they may just *think* that they are now the man of the house.

It could be really helpful to have conversations with your children about the dynamics in the family and how they have changed with one of the parents no longer there (see 5.1 for more information around this subject).

This section is about the role figure and how to reassure adults to be adults and children to remain as children.

I would like you to ask yourself, what does it mean for you, if you say to your child that they are now the man of the house? What does it feel like to not have a 'man of the house'? What role does the man of the house have?

Yes, I do understand that you may be feeling a loss of no longer having your partner with you and to have another person allocated that role may make you feel more secure or not alone.

What I would like you to consider is: what task(s)/role did your partner fulfil and can you identify any other adults that could take on some of those task(s)/roles. Be it friends or other family members. Or is there something DIY wise etc. that you may need to learn or be taught. If so, do you know who could show you how to do that task?

When we say to a young person, "You are now the man of the house," whilst the child might feel proud of being given such a role, they also might feel the burden and responsibility of what comes with it. How do other siblings feel about the brother becoming the man of the house, what does it mean for them? The brother may not be the oldest and yet in their older sibling's eyes, they may feel they have been rewarded or given seniority over them.

You may not realise it yet, but the child that has become 'the man of the house' may feel they can't go out with their friends because you need them at home.

Whilst you are all adapting to the changes and loss of the previous family setup, it is important for your child to have that opportunity too. It is important for them to be able to make sense of their own feelings as a child, and the impact that it has had/is having on them.

You may not have a partner at the moment or a partner that yet lives with you. Maybe the thought of that may make you shudder or say 'no way', or 'not yet', or 'I can't even begin to imagine that' and that's ok. However what if one day that does happen, then suddenly, for example, you may now have the situation of 'two males of the house' and that does not bode well.

You may find that your child wants to take on some of the chores, which your previous partner undertook. I think it could be helpful to acknowledge their offer and ask them about their thinking behind it.

We may not be aware or even realise it, but children can try and rescue parents, when there has been a separation. They may want to fill the void that they have perceived and they may want to 'make it better' for you.

Imagine your partner was controlling in your relationship. They still could be giving money, sharing your child etc. Now that they are no longer living with you, you may want to do things your way for the time being. As an example; your previous partner used to walk the dog and your child is offering to do so, however *you* would like to walk the dog and that is ok.

You may decide to share out some of the chores, and if you have more than one child and to create a healthy balance, they could do a particular chore on alternate weeks.

Before deciding any of those things though, do give yourself time to ask 'If a partner comes into my life or starts living with me, would I like them to do that'? This doesn't mean that if that is the case you need to still do it all, but again to be mindful of any future changes in daily chores and the impact that may have.

Separations affect everyone in their own way. Upon a rupture happening, the next stage is to recreate/find a solid foundation again. The feeling of being 'safe' is paramount, even if you may not consciously be thinking that, your subconscious definitely will.

Therefore, aiming to give a child something i.e., a chore or responsibility, only to take it away again would not be conducive for that young person. This will cause a further rupture for your child.

I have mentioned chores, however the most natural way

that a child becomes a role figure is through communication. They may become the one that you speak to, when you are feeling sad or angry. It may be just the two of you at home and therefore, it may seem obvious/natural to talk to your child about how you are feeling about the situation. *Remember my sister's situation [pg. 37].*

I am aware that as a parent you may not intentionally create this role figure in your child, but it may happen gradually over time. For instance, it might be a Saturday evening, where you and your Ex used to watch a film together. You may then ask your child to watch a film with you, when actually the child wants to be gaming with their friends. Your child may protest and without realising it you could find yourself saying, "But I'm lonely" or "what about your poor mum/dad?".

There could be times when you have a dilemma or want to talk something through and again you turn to your child. Remember all the time you are a parent your child is always your child, no matter what age they are.

Whether your child sees their other parent or not, being involved in 'adult' conversations can make the child feel awkward when they next see their other parent. Or they may feel the need to report back to you when they have spent time with their other parent. This can cause a great deal of conflict for your child.

I think what also needs to be recognised is that a child could become a role figure or be treated more like an adult at either home, which again can cause disruption to the alternate home where they spend time in. It could turn into a 'Well Dad treats me like an adult, why don't you?' – situation. (See more in-depth information surrounding this in 4.1.)

Your child more than likely is never going to say to you directly, don't treat me like an adult or challenge what you might talk about to them. Firstly, they will not want to upset you or offend, and secondly, they may find it incredibly uncomfortable and indeed challenging for themselves.

In that instance I would say notice their body language. Are they walking away whilst you are trying to talk to them, or are they distracting themselves? They may not be able to look you in the eye, as it could feel too much for them. Your child will definitely be giving you signals.

This could include returning back from the other parent's home and going up to their room for a while. On the other hand, this time could be helping them either acclimatise back to where they are now, or simply to avoid a potential barrage of questions.

Ask your child how they want to manage integrating between the two homes. You may feel it is showing an interest asking your child question about what they have been up to? Which, yes, it could be, but your child may find it awkward and interrogating, or indeed a way to have a go at that parent!

7.4. GPS – Guilty Parent Syndrome

This is not to be confused with a *satnav*! Although, a bit like a *satnav*, when you press the home button, *this* GPS always takes you to the same place too.

So, what is guilty parent syndrome? This is not a bona fide term, but purely a term I made up, as I have seen it so many times. Both in client sessions and personally. I have witnessed it being acted out, and I have seen how children use it to the 'best' of their ability.

Guilty parent syndrome is when a parent feels guilty about the breakup of their relationship with the other parent, whether or not it might have been in the interests of the family.

A parent, who no longer lives with their child, may have a strong GPS signal, but what tends to happen is that the *instigating* parent of the separation in some way feels, they may have let their child down. Hence they need to somehow compensate their child. Although I must point out, that either parent can at times have GPS.

When a parent does compensate, it can be to the detriment to other members of the family.

Let's look at an example; you have your child every other weekend or say once a month. Imagine you have already tentatively planned, what you would like to do that weekend. This could be including your new partner and or the other children living in the home.

However, when your child arrives and they learn of what has been planned but share that they do not want to do that, as the part-time parent, your GPS might kick in around now. You may find yourself considering changing the plans as you could have an urge to 'make it better' for your child whom is only with you for the weekend.

A parent experiencing GPS could include changing plans, dipping out of the plans already agreed, so that they and their child can do something that the child wants. The parent may desperately feel that the plans need to change in order that their child will be happy or to have a 'successful' weekend with them.

The GPS can cause great aggravation (spoken and unspoken) within the home and indeed between partners. You may feel that you don't have GPS, but your partner may think otherwise.

You may be able to justify what you do by saying to yourself, 'Of course I want them to have a good time when they visit me', or 'I don't see them that often'. But, if you were to ask yourself is the relationship balanced when they come to stay, and if you answer honestly, it may provide you with a hint as to whether you have GPS.

You may (or may not) notice that the weekend completely revolves around your child, what you do, what you have for food, what TV is watched for example. Yes, I am sure your child is having a great time to a degree, but what about you?

You may not consider about their other home, but can I ask you to consider what happens when your child returns and has to rearrange themselves as they may not be the main focus of attention?

GPS is not helpful for you or your child going forward. Without realising, your GPS is creating an unwritten contract between you.

You may ask yourself, what is an unwritten contract? An unwritten contract is something that can happen between two people subconsciously.

For example, in the instance of your child having two homes, it could be: when they come to yours, the first thing to happen is they are given sweets. This becomes the unwritten contract, because that is what always happens.

Potentially later on, you may decide the sweets are too expensive, or they are not eating their dinner as a result of too many sweets. Your GPS signal will be so strong and could cause you quite a lot of angst if you were to go against what you have always done.

If you decide to make this change, this could disrupt your relationship with your child, which you may feel even more guilty, and so the cycle clicks back into place and continues.

But all is not lost!

First of all, it may be helpful to try a bird's-eye-view of the situation. Write down how your time with your child normally looks. I am not asking you to justify why you do whatever you do, I am just suggesting, that you write down bullet points of what a weekend or day generally looks like.

Then, I would like you to notice how you feel about *how* you spend your time with your child. You will probably say to make them happy or to create memories, which I do understand, but let's ask it in a different way. How might you feel if you didn't fulfil all the wants of your child but do some of things you may like to do also?

Having a balanced relationship with your child is important for both of you and for your child growing up. It allows your child to learn to be considerate of others, it enables you to consider yourself too. It also allows you to break those 'contracts', which are not helpful or healthy to any party concerned.

The age of your child will influence how you change your contract. If they are old enough, you can sit down with them and explain that the weekend is a treat and opportunity for both of you. Hence, you can both make choices about arrangements even down to the choice of food/meals etc. It is of the upmost importance for children to learn the nature of compromise.

If the contract has been going on for quite some time, and they have begun to expect that's how it is, then you may choose to do it gradually. Every other week you could change the breakfast, lunch or dinner to not necessarily suit your child's wishes, or preferences – again compromise.

You may have older children whom you do not see that regularly, however they seem to contact you when they need something. Again it may be helpful to meet up with them or if texting is your method of communication, then text them to say what you will be changing, or what you would like from the relationship.

If possible, you may feel able to 'name it', that you feel they only contact you when they want something. Yes, it may feel uncomfortable, however again, you are teaching them really healthy ways to communicate.

GPS is a completely natural behavioural pattern, but it doesn't actually favour or teach anybody anything! Like all contracts, there are loopholes and it can take time to get out of and GPS is no different. It will take time and hard work, and at times feel easier to revert back to how it used to be.

However, freeing yourself from the GPS could actually enhance your relationship with your child in the long run. This may allow you to be you and to consider yourself. Be ok with your child fitting in with your new family or lifestyle.

If you notice that your child acts in a particular way when they are with you or expects certain things, talk to them about it. Sometimes them asking for something else could actually be their way of reassuring themselves, that they do matter or that you do care. They are possibly reaffirming to themselves, that they haven't been 'forgotten' in your new relationship.

When your children are involved in the separation of parents, they are trying to make sense of what is happening, and more often than not their addings-up may not make the right equation. They may also have heard 'adult only' comments about their parents. This creates a need for them to prove what they heard wasn't right. It's really important that you talk to them, find out what is going on for them.

You never know, they may feel guilty that they don't live with you, and therefore go along with everything you suggest to keep you happy. GPS can work both ways.

I moved home a while ago, and I couldn't believe the amount of people that 'trusted' their *satnav* even though the road sign to our new home says Close. Which I believe fundamentally means no access to other roads. People still turned into the road to use as a 'cut through'.

Due to the continuous stream of traffic, an additional sign was put up saying 'No Through Road', yet still drivers either ignored or blindly handed over their common sense to their *satnav*.

It's almost like they've relinquished any responsibility or decision-making about where they are going and for me this also feels like GPS (no pun intended) when it comes to parenting. They dissolve any common sense and end up down a very single-minded track, which isn't healthy for the parties concerned; both parents and children.

8. Different Ways To Have A Conversation

As I mentioned in the introduction and continue to reiterate throughout this book, good communication is really the king or queen of words.

Whether we are communicating about how we feel (yikes that feeling word again!) or communicating about chores to be completed at home and everything in between, we are always communicating.

What makes this chapter different is for you to look at the many different ways of communicating, and also what could be communicated, and what may be best left unsaid or at least worded differently.

There will probably have been and also will be in the future, times when people have expressed that they know *exactly* how you feel, but actually they don't! Yes, they may have separated or divorced, yes, their child could be driving them mad and yes, possibly their in-laws irritate them too. BUT the fundamental difference is, *they* are not you!

Bear in mind the different types of learning styles people have, visual, auditory, reading/writing and kinaesthetic (the definition of kinaesthetic is being tactile, i.e. by doing something by hand yourself, for example making the bread as opposed to watching someone make the bread).

That *alone* shows you how individual we are. I have already shared that I am personally a visual learner followed immediately by kinaesthetic. This way of learning could also be used, when we are communicating. We will all have our preferred ways of communicating for either a) to certain people and b) and about certain subjects.

To start with, you may use a certain method within your new adapted family, such as a *WhatsApp* group. As communication between yourselves becomes more comfortable the group chat may be used less and less. Maybe face-to-face communication is more common.

However, if you feel communication seems to have taken a dive, you could stop it from going any further and reopen the app again – send a message out – saying you feel communication has gone a bit awry and what are their thoughts on this?

Being a good communicator is a great trait to have and yet it needs to be worked on constantly, as it most likely doesn't come like second nature. You and the other members of your family (and yes that does include your Ex) need to all work on it too!

The great thing with learning to be a good communicator, is that it can become a good habit.

Good communication actually relieves stress and tension, as you will tend to no longer hold onto gripes or whatever it might be that frustrates you, but instead communicating how you are feeling to the parties involved – result!

Like all good habits, communication takes practise, practise, *practise* – but you will get there and you will reap the benefits. I endorse this 100%.

8.1. Walking, driving, texting, communication book

The most important part is not giving up – it may take time.

Sometimes a proven method could get stuck, and so you may have to learn to unstick it. You may also come to the conclusion that a particular communication method no longer works.

I have seen wonderful things flourish when communication is present.

There really are endless ways of communicating and what may work for one parent/child may be completely different for another and that's ok! As I said in the opening paragraph, it's about NOT giving up.

I remember working with a client, who was desperately trying to communicate with their dad and in the end it turned out that texting was the key to open communication. For another walking the dog with their mum proved fruitful for communicating with each other. For both sets of people, their communication methods provided them with the space for individually 'being heard'.

You as a parent may feel frustrated and desperate to speak to your child, but *your* chosen method of communication may feel too intense or judgemental for your child.

Your child may already feel that you have made your mind up before hearing and listening to *them*. Or, that you don't actually believe it's them, the child that are saying that, but instead it is the other parent that has 'engineered' what your child is trying to say.

If you think about how young people connect in today's world, it is predominantly *social media*. So for them to communicate via a device can make total sense in their world.

Over the years, my stepdaughter and I have had our challenges. I believe a lot has been due to outside pressures and the amazing (said slightly sarcastically) 'shoulds' and the 'oughts'.

The good thing is, is that we are always able to reconnect via text, texting allows us to be our true selves to one another. When I receive a text from her, it makes me smile inwards and outwards. Also when we converse in this way it reminds me of the relationship we used to have.

Texting could also include having a *WhatsApp* group, where your child may text both parents for example. Please do not make decisions about who *could* be in that group without discussing it with your child. They may not want stepparents in a certain group, or their other parent or siblings.

Remember, whilst it may not seem private, it does provide a private space for them to be heard, and for them to address any concerns or worries they may have. Be respectful and you will not only gain respect back from your child, but this will also give them the foundations for trust, acceptance and being heard. Which believe me is a HUGE thing! (More about being heard in the next section 8.2.)

Before we look at the different ways of communication, please bear in mind what may work for you may not necessarily work for your child. The fact they want to communicate is a bonus – stick with it! Even if you need to recognise that their way of communicating isn't what you may want. However it is how they wish to do it and that's the key here.

So, let us take a walk through communication;

Talking: Ok, this could be a variety of ways, it could be sitting in the room together. I appreciate in my counselling sessions we face one another, but this may feel too intense or restrictive.

So perhaps you could sit next to each other (no eye-to-eye contact) and maybe have the TV on, as that can help reduce what may feel like an intense situation for either or both of you.

Maybe if you are cooking this could feel easier for your child, almost 'talking to your back' could feel less intimidating. This way they may not be feeling scrutinised by you or see your facial gestures, as they say what they need to say. Whilst you may feel, that you are being open and listening to them, your face (and body for that matter) may say a thousand different words.

Going for a walk. Again, you would be walking side-by-side which could feel more comfortable. The walk could provide distractions. You are out in public, so potentially this could avoid no loud outbursts or shouting (hopefully!). Your child may be worried about you shouting and walking outside could prevent this.

You don't have to have a dog, but if you do this will add another positive distraction. If for instance your child started to feel uncomfortable, they could throw a ball or chase the dog, which could provide an opportunity of some much-needed time out.

Driving can also be a positive way of communicating. Again, you are both facing the same direction. You may or may not have music playing and providing you are not caught up in traffic, the motion of the car could prove to be quite soothing – remember how babies and people in general can nod off when being driven.

Over the phone. Whilst this may seem obvious, again, it will create a form of distance or separation between the two of you. Remember to pay attention to your tone and your expressions should you be using *FaceTime*, as these will be seen and heard – loud and clear. Also, be ok if your child does not want to *FaceTime,* maybe they aren't ready to do that even if they seem to do it all the time with their friends.

I would encourage you to sit/walk with any uncomfortable feelings you may be having as you are the adult here. If you notice you want to interrupt or defend yourself – STOP – let your child finish talking – THEN – consider what they have just said, not what you *think*, they have just said.

Texting: As I mentioned earlier, this could be normal text, *WhatsApp* or any other app they may choose. A key thing about *WhatsApp* in particular is that (if the settings allow), you can see when the other person was last online, or whether they have read your text or not.

DO NOT and I repeat DO NOT get too hung up on that, if you have responded to their last communication and can see they've been online and either have or haven't read your text be patient and wait – give them space.

Communication book: The way this book works is that you or your child may write how they are feeling or concerned about something. The person who wrote that may be able to articulate how they would like the other person to hear them. They may also suggest what they need to help look at what is concerning them.

Be aware of always leaving the book in a place that has been agreed. If you feel that no one else could come across it, then it could be left on the kitchen work surface.

Ideally this will be in a mutually convenient place and ideally not in either of your own personal bedrooms. Otherwise your child could misconstrue this and think that you are using it as an excuse to be in their room, to potentially 'check-up' on them.

Once you or your child have either read or responded, the communication book will then be placed back in the agreed 'safe place'. If there is nothing to be said, the communication book can sit in the 'safe place' until such times as it is needed.

Remember all of these methods will generally be per child if you have more than one. You may have a family *WhatsApp* group, but the individual ones are exactly that *individual*.

Like I said and keep saying, try different things. Sometimes one way may work for a while but could peter out. A previously tried method that didn't work initially, may work a second or third time round.

You may feel your communication method(s) are hopeless, but this could have been down to how your child responded? Maybe you felt they were negative and therefore your defences may have gone up.

Initially the main thing to do is to 'play' with the idea together. There is no right or wrong way, it's your ways. Yes, you may at times feel frustrated by this method, but when it works, it works, and then you may feel relief that your child is now communicating with you rather than maybe what feels like grunting or not saying anything at all – that is what I call a win–win!

Build trust, respect and a listening ear and you can open up a great communication method with your child – I can assure you – invest in it and you will both reap the rewards.

8.2. Listen and communicate: what did you just hear?

I see this so many times in and out of the counselling room. It is amazing how someone can say something between two people, and yet what they have just said appears to have got lost in translation.

Before you grab hold of this life-changing tool (which I personally feel it is), next time you are standing in a queue or around other people, notice when one person speaks, how the other person that they were talking to hasn't heard them. Or you may even notice it in conversations you have with other people.

We live in a very, very busy world, and we have almost everything at our fingertips. If we choose to, we can be contacted 24/7 pretty much (give or take a phone signal) anywhere. Whilst we may not be consciously aware of our phones or other devices, our subconscious probably is. We have one ear on the present and one ear 'listening' out for the phone notifying us, of whatever it might be.

As I said, life is busy, and we can have all sorts of different situations going on in our daily lives. This is not about being mindful or present all the time (that's probably another book!). Mindfulness in this situation is about being *present* when you are communicating with your child.

You may jump to your defence and say that you are present, well, being in the same room, car, or walking with them makes you physically present but not necessarily mindfully and emotionally present. You could be thinking about what to do for dinner, about an email that you need to send or chase up. A conversation you had with someone else could be playing on your mind or not wanting to be late back because of X, Y and Z. You may even be on your device!

So, let us look at how to listen and communicate. I apologise now, if you feel like I am teaching you to suck eggs (which by the way, is a saying that I have never understood).

The way this works is really simple and powerful, if you choose to learn it. Need I say more?

Ok, let me give you an example: your child may say they don't want to go to their other parent's home this evening. It is changeover day or they always go to their parent's house on this night, or it has been arranged for this evening.

You may say, "Why ever not, you always enjoy yourself when you get there" or "That's what's been arranged." However you may respond, you may feel equally pleased that is 'one up' to you as they don't want to go to their other parents.

I totally understand, that you may have been holding on to this evening, a break, a glimmer of light for you to have a 'night off' or whatever it may mean to you. However right now, I need you to park your feelings and wants not because you don't count, you do, but you need to find out the reason for your child's comment.

So, like I said, none of the above is the point, the point is your child has said they don't want to go to their other parent's house.

I am going to ask you to repeat your childs words back to them, but before you do, please keep your tone level and your body language mutual, regardless of how you are feeling to what they have just said.

In an ideal world, I would like you to repeat back almost exactly what they said, "You don't want to go to your dad's/ mum's this evening?" (Full stop). Please refrain from saying anything else, or adding anything else, or putting what you think into the mix. And now for what might feel like the difficult bit – pause.

Give your child the space to say what is going on for them. Again, when they speak, repeat back what you have just heard. I appreciate you may feel like a parrot or a robot but for your child, they will hear that you have heard them, you are using their words not yours.

NEVER underestimate the power of hearing your own words spoken back to you.

Once your child has shared what is going on for them, ask them what they would like to do. I know they said they didn't want to go, but your conversation may have allowed them to express, how they are feeling and are now able to look at the situation differently as opposed to being overridden or dismissed.

This is how listening and hearing what has been said works.

To start with, I would highly recommend practising this but with general things and with anyone.

For example, imagine you say "Wow what a beautiful day." Ask the person that you are with what you just said, see if they actually say "You said it's a beautiful day" or whether they interpreted that to be whatever they *thought* you said, or they thought they *heard* you say. On the other hand, notice when someone else says something and how you have interpreted what they are saying.

When we stop second-guessing or putting our wants and needs in the middle of what we may have heard, it can basically make life a little easier. This way of communicating enables us to see the comments for what they are and where those comments are originating from.

It never ceases to amaze me when I work with couples or a young person and their parent, how this presents itself. When I ask either party, what they have just heard, I am intrigued (that's my job), by their interpretation.

A classic response is, "That's not really what they mean, they're just saying that cos you're in the room." Or the other person says something that I certainly didn't hear and none of the other person's words are repeated at all.

However, like all things this takes practise and with this new-found tool, you can also ask your child what did they just hear – it works both ways.

I encourage you to practise this on what I would call non-trivial matters. The reason for this, is that this is giving everyone the opportunity to practice saying, "What did you just hear?" You and your child will change from responding with what you thought you heard to what you actually did hear.

If you were to test this on something that has great importance to you, you may well feel offended, upset or angry because there is a looming disappointment of not being heard. You may already be thinking of times, when you have not been heard or how often you have felt unheard. In a way, I would be pleased to hear this, as you yourself will recognise how important it is to be *heard*!

Sometimes just being heard is enough, there may be no further action required. Being heard allows us to feel important and noticed and that our feelings and thoughts count.

Another way to respond for example is if someone was to say, "I am feeling sad." Here you could reply by saying, "I hear you are feeling sad." That sentence literally says I have heard what you have said.

When people tell us things, we may feel an urge to make it right or fix it. This could be because you haven't learnt to really listen, or because what they are saying may feel upsetting or uncomfortable for you. However this isn't about you, it's about them. SO, as best as you can, sit with the potentially, uncomfortable, awkward or non-fixing approach.

9. The Ex!

I wonder how many of you will consider skipping this section, as the idea of even 'going there' causes too great a reaction?

I would really encourage you to read this section. I cannot stress the importance of any relationship between estranged parents and the impact that this can have on your child.

I expect you are already answering me back with your reasons and experiences of how this subject leaves you feeling. I am in no way discrediting how you feel, or telling you not to feel like that. I am also certainly not preaching to you.

However exactly how you may be feeling about your Ex right now as we start to tiptoe over the topic, these feelings will definitely be being picked up by your child – even if they aren't being vocalised (as per chapter 7, 'Take Responsibility'). It is not ok for your child to be included in *your* stuff about *your* Ex.

Like it or not, you will always be 'part of the Ex'. Whether your child does or does not have a relationship with their other parent, they were at some point in their life (and could still be) a significant person. Yes, even if the relationship was not a healthy one, that parent will forever have a place in your child's mind and archive of memories – good or bad.

Your child may or may not choose to talk about their other parent in your presence, or maybe the silence is their chatter?

At the end of the day all the parties involved in the separation/divorce and new families are all *people*. They are all unique individuals all with their own idiosyncrasies.

So no, you and your Ex won't probably always get it right, BUT trying to make it easier for your child and putting your stuff to one side (for adult ears only) is a really positive step.

Imagine this; you have a friend who features heavily in your life, maybe she is always popping in to see you, or you generally meet up when you're out shopping. Now imagine that your child really doesn't like this friend, they find them irritating or say boring. So when you mention them coming round or meeting up in town, your child shares their disgruntlement or start to make it awkward or unpleasant for you – get the idea?

Ok, I would like you to now notice how you might feel about that situation. You may start to feel annoyed towards your child, because what that person brings feels like the only positive highlight in your life right now. You may feel challenged by their behaviour, although you are the adult here. Whatever feelings you could have about your child's reaction – your child will have their own feelings too about how you 'manage' your Ex.

So please, bear with me and read this chapter, if not for you but for your child.

9.1. Stop slating your Ex to your child

Probably by the time you have reached this chapter and possibly, months before, you did exactly that, badmouth your Ex to your child. Or perhaps in the vicinity of your child.

If you are now thinking about the times that you did badmouth your Ex. Can I ask you to reflect on what you said, and then I would like you to apologise to your child. Explain that you have been thinking about things that you have said in the past, and that it wasn't right or ok and that you are sorry – accept responsibility.

I realise this may feel uncomfortable, I would like you to ask your child if there is anything that they would like to say on the matter. This conversation may come as a surprise to them and they may need to process what you have just said. In this case let them know, that they can come back to you to talk about anything, they might want to.

This is the first step in reclaiming what was your stuff and not theirs.

I do understand that at times you may not feel you have anyone to turn to, or your child has just walked into the room following a heated telephone conversation with your Ex. That still doesn't make it ok to sound off to them. This could be tearing their mum or dad apart, or sharing information about their parent, which they would never normally have known about, had you both have stayed together.

I have worked with a whole range of age groups. With the majority of my clients that have been involved in parents separating or not getting on, they have been told things that quite frankly they never wanted to know. Believe me, this is not my clients wanting to put their head in the sand – they simply did not want to know.

Let's look at this way, would you want to hear the 'ins and outs' of their friendships? I think probably not, so why would your child want to know yours?

You may feel that there would be no point in dragging up things that you have previously said and apologised for. However I am all too aware of the relief they will feel if you acknowledge that it was never meant to be shared with them. This way they no longer have to harbour any feelings attached to what was said and also what hasn't been said.

Yes, there will always be two sides to every story, they may never get to hear the other side (admittedly they probably don't want to know). However that won't stop them filling in the blanks and creating their own stories on behalf of the other parent. This is not helpful or healthy for anyone especially your child.

To help you manage your feelings about your Ex, why not set up a *WhatsApp* group with some friends who are willing to be a sounding off board. If you need to sound off send an uncensored message, and let your friends be there for you.

Alternatively, you could write down how you are feeling or what you would like to say. Failing everything else there is always screaming into your pillow! I cannot stress the importance of 'getting it out', literally extracting your feelings. Although, they need to be channelled in the most appropriate adult way.

Your child will see you suffer and they will offer to be your pillar of strength, but this is not what should be the case because they are *your child*.

I appreciate this may sound like I am back on my soapbox, but I am so acutely aware in both my private and professional arenas, of the impact in hearing these interactions.

During my parents' divorce my youngest sibling was feeling being 'dragged' around during the very acrimonious divorce. Due to my youngest sibling being exactly that, they were too young to be left at home. Instead they were subjected to hearing adult conversations, which should never have taken place anywhere near them.

If you have a friend or family member over and you want to share something or talk about how you are feeling, you may have to wait until another time. Or arrange to see them when you have the house to yourself, or when your child is at school. Talking in hushed voices or with the door closed, or stopping talking altogether when your child enters the room will only have a negative effect for your child.

If I could just press pause right here… can I ask you to imagine at the age that you are now, if you were to experience any of those situations, how could this make you feel?

When I consider how I might feel, I would definitely feel vulnerable, possibly that I had done something wrong or indeed something not very nice was going to happen. I know for sure that I would be feeling excluded and possibly worried.

Now, I would like you to consider the age of your child and hopefully that may give you an idea of the impact of how an adult conversation that is quickly stopped or hushed may have on *them*.

There are so many things that can be thrown into this section, your Ex may or may not have had an affair. As they don't want to look like the 'bad' parent, they may start telling lies to your child about you. As hard as it may be to remain cool in this situation, take a deep breath and listen to your child. Take a little time out and then speak to them (depending on how you are feeling). Calmly explain to them that it isn't ok for the parent to be saying anything unhelpful to them. Reassure them that this is not for them to worry about and they have done nothing wrong.

Your Ex could be bitter, but ultimately this is neither your stuff nor your child's.

An exercise that you may find helpful to do, is:

Imagine your Ex has just 'metaphorically' handed you a bag of rubbish (their rubbish). You take their bag of rubbish and glance at it. (Glance is the significant word here.) Ok, as you glanced at the bag, you remember that it isn't your rubbish, but your Ex's.

However they have driven off and left you with it, so I would like you to imagine placing it (or throwing it, if that helps) in the household waste bin outside. It has to be the household waste bin, as we do not want their 'rubbish' to be recycled.

What you are doing here, is recognising whose 'rubbish' is whose and disposing of the rubbish nonetheless and not taking any of it on board!

I remember working with a client whose Ex chose to leave them. Later as it appeared not to be working out, how the Ex-partner had envisaged, they became very bitter and were quite demonstrative in their actions, words and behaviours towards my client.

My client smiled and said "You must be bitter cos you eat so many lemons." My client said that with a smile on their face, as there was no malice. This way we both managed to smile, in what was a really difficult time for my client. Can you see, how my client, didn't accept their Ex's rubbish but mildly acknowledged it.

At all times where possible, try to and 'play nicely'. Censoring your thoughts and words in front of your child will be positive for now and in the future.

I am aware that it is perfectly ok for me to be shouting about a sibling or relative of mine to my husband. However, if he were to talk negatively of them or join in with my rant, I would swiftly change tactics and defend said sibling or relative. This is how a young person may feel too.

Hearing and witnessing negative communication and actions between parents can leave your child feeling very emotionally confused. You are both still their parents at the end of the day and seeing you two in conflict, can lead them to question where they sit amongst this debris of a family.

Remember how I repeatedly express the importance of communication? Well, we want to encourage your child to open up and talk, not close them down.

Your child may feel unsure whether to share anything that has happened at their other home in case it is used against that parent or indeed that the other parent hears about it and scolds them for telling. Their world already feels unsafe with their parents living apart and the challenges that this can bring.

Therefore it is important to make them feel 'OK' in whichever home they are in and with whichever parent. Otherwise this can lead to your child taking sides or feeling they should (see 15.1) take sides.

This is not *their* battle. Not only will they be dealing with their own turmoil regarding their parents' separation, but also the regular day-to-day things that a young person/adult has to manage. So it would be helpful for them not take on their parents' turmoil too.

A good thing to remember is there isn't a 'good cop' or a 'bad cop'. They NEED consistent cops (plural).

10. The New Relationship

This chapter is about you and your new partner. For further reading on your new *family* (see 11).

When you enter a new relationship, or start entertaining the idea of having a new partner, be aware of the 'shoulds'. The 'shoulds' from both yourself and others, i.e., friends.

So, what could the 'shoulds' look like? Well it could be you asking yourself, 'Should I be waiting longer before I enter another relationship?' On the hand people may say, "You should be thinking of you and your child right now, you haven't got time for a new relationship!"

To understand more about how the 'shoulds' work see (15).

So let us look at your question to yourself; 'Should I be waiting longer before I enter another relationship?' I knew a friend who was seeing a counsellor and this friend was concerned about it being too soon to be in a relationship. Their counsellor, who I hold in very high regard said, "But you've never been in a relationship, so why would it be too soon?"

This resounded for my friend, and the 'should' dissolved into, I 'could' enter this relationship. I feel that was a really healthy way of looking at their situation. Just because we are deemed to be in a 'relationship', it doesn't necessarily mean we are, or that the relationship is a mutually beneficial one. This, I feel is very good 'food for thought'.

Just to further clarify, you may initially have been in a relationship with your partner, but things may have drifted, communication has gone awry, intimacy may have faded etc., so then what did you have left that constituted a relationship, or indeed were these ever there in the first place?

Since hearing the counsellor's comment, I have been able to explore this with my clients when they too were asking the same question.

These are a few things that can happen when people form a new relationship;

People rush to get approval from their friends/family and, not listen to their own gut feeling. People try to 'shoehorn' their new partner into every day daily life. And lastly, people can forget to enjoy the here-and-now, live-in-the-moment opportunities with their new partner.

Why would you rush this?

This initial stage in your relationship is irreplaceable and unique to you both, so cherish it and dare I say, indulge in it. Use this treasured time to grow as a couple together and what I feel, most importantly, is learn to be 'interdependent'. Interdependent means, still being your own person whilst incorporating *part* of yourselves into your relationship.

Imagine two circles where one is drawn so it equally overlaps the other one. The 'non-overlapping' sections on each side are you and your partner (separately/dependent). Such as you doing a hobby, sport or seeing your friends. The middle part is you both in the relationship (doing things together). That's what interdependent could look like. (For us visual learners!)

People can be too quick to compromise to the detriment of themselves. This can later easily turn into resentment.

No matter how keen you might be for your child to meet your new partner, or indeed they may have got a sense that you have someone new in their life,

Do. Not. Rush. It.

Let's look at this another way; I have no idea whether you are a gardener or not, but again, I ask you to bear with me and imagine this:

You have just got your first allotment. It didn't come easy, you were on numerous waiting lists for several months, if not years. For the first time, you excitedly visit your allotment.

When you arrive, you realise before you can plant anything, you need to do some planning.

You may need a shed for your tools (which are yet to be bought), somewhere to put your flask and sandwiches for the days that you imagine spending time here. Before you purchase your shed, you will work out the best place for it to be positioned. You will consider, based on where the sun falls and how you imagine your allotment will look, where you will place your shed and what size you will want/need.

Whilst you are waiting for your shed to be delivered or collected, you start measuring out the area of your allotment. You may have even spoken to several other owners of allotments there too, to get their views and knowledge of what has worked and not worked for them. They may have given you advice about soil etc.

Over the next few weeks (depending on what time of year it is), you may be mulling over how it is going to look, or start digging the soil over, doing as much preparation 'to give your flowers, fruit and vegetables the best start as possible'.

All of this 'preparation' will ideally be to help you get the best harvest or most enjoyment from your allotment. Yes, you may make mistakes we are 'only human' after all. I imagine, if you haven't gone all 'gung-ho', then you may in time reap the rewards.

Bearing the allotment in mind, I then ask you to ask yourself, why wouldn't you do this with your new relationship and in turn potential new family?

So, I will repeat once more; Do. Not. Rush. It.

10.1. Your child is playing catch-up

As an adult you need your own support network, children cannot be your crutch no matter what age they are. They are dealing with their own feelings and managing *their* take on the situation.

For your child, you will be part of their support network. But try and consider who else can they talk to. Is there a teacher or counsellor at school, an adult friend or relative whom you know they get on with? It may even be their best friend's mum/dad.

A child may want to know what's going on, it's probably not to do with being nosey, but the breakup may be unexpected, and it may be a shock to them. Now they do not want to potentially feel like they are being kept in the dark, as they will understandably feel vulnerable.

If the separation felt like it came out of the blue, their natural instinct will now be in survival mode, on high alert, as their secure base may no longer feel safe. Whilst reading that, you may feel I'm exaggerating, but depending on which 'position' you were in regarding the separation, that may have been your experience too.

You were either the person choosing to leave and hence aware your relationship was coming to an end or potentially you had no idea either. To elaborate on the 'no idea either' scenario: you could also finally have uncovered your partners longstanding affair and have found that you are actually the last person to know. Or, they may have been running a double life – this is more common than we may think.

Let's look at these individually:

Choosing to leave: how did you feel knowing that? Did you need to get out of the relationship because it was abusive which may mean leaving the children behind for the time being whilst you make alternative housing arrangements?

Is there another adult involved and therefore you feel, you may have someone to help you through the breakup? How long has this been going on for you, months, years? How many times in your head have you tried to leave? Have you tried to live as though everything is ok, and keep everything 'normal' in the home? Did you have a friend or friends to talk to about wanting to leave?

Basically, think about how you feel about the breakup now, compared to when you realised it was over. Now, whilst potentially still feeling sad, you may be relieved that you can now 'get on with your life'. Initially you may naturally have felt overwhelmed with the thought of breaking up the family.

Feeling that the relationship is coming to an end: you may have been 'happy' with the relationship ticking over. For example, due to financial constraints or not being able to see life beyond the relationship. It could be that you feel it is glaringly obvious that you and your partner are no longer in love and for you, enough is enough and it's time to go your own separate ways.

Again, was there any reason for your child to be aware that you and your partner are not getting along? You may both have made the effort at weekends when the family was together at home, or only did family things together for the sake of the children.

This is where the vulnerability for the children can kick in, because their world seemed to be ok and ticking along nicely. This 'fake relationship' could cause a rupture in their minds as to doubt what is real and what isn't.

If you had no idea either – as a young person they see their parent(s) as the protector and if your child realises that you (the parent) didn't see it coming then your child could feel incredibly unsafe. Maybe your shock and upset is preventing them for sharing how they feel, thinking you have enough on your plate without having to deal with their own turmoil, or your child is now putting on a brave face for mummy or daddy or both!

One thing you may find helpful could be literally getting down to their level and trying to see it from the child's point of view. If necessary, take yourself down to their height by sitting on your knees, if they are at school or out, sit in their bedroom, see their world. If you had planned leaving your partner and have somewhere to go and are taking your child, your child (along with yourself) is being uprooted.

I never forget transplanting an acer when we moved. I thought you could just dig it up from one garden and plant it in the new one, but according to our very knowledgeable gardener that was not the case.

The plant had to live in the pot it was transported in, because the plants memory still thought it was in the old ground. It needed to allow its roots to grow and it took 8–9 months before it was ok for it to be replanted – 8–9 months!! What's more, it can take up to two years after it has been planted in the ground for us to know whether it has survived or not.

Not that I'm dissing plants, but if that's the impact on a plant being uprooted or having its established home being changed, then understandably the impact on the family and their members could also be seismic too.

This potentially may sound like I'm a 'know-it-all' gardener, which I do not profess to be at all, however I believe I may have read somewhere… that when someone moves into a new home it is advisable to leave both the home and garden for a year before doing anything major. This gives you the chance to get a feel for the home and see what you might like to do, it also enables you to see your home and garden through the four seasons and what might work in the summer might not be so great in the winter.

I feel this is a good starting point when you separate, as much as you may want to 'rip it up and start again', how about giving yourself and your child time to settle and get used to the new family arrangements?

If you want to rearrange the furniture, let your child know this is your plan, even if you do it whilst they are at school, by communicating this to them at least they will be expecting it. Or tell them about it when you pick them up, again this is sharing the information with them so that they do not feel like they are in the dark, again.

So, going forward, when you notice there is going to potentially be another change, allow yourself time to see, how this would work for all the other members in the home. Could this affect changeover days, or clubs that your child attends? Who benefits from the change and how?

Giving yourself the space to look at this from different angles will enable you to decide how you may want to bring up the subject. Also as mentioned before speak to friends or family or your counsellor about any concerns you have.

I am by no means saying not to change anything. I am just suggesting for you to consider all angles, the impact and how to *communicate* it to your child.

Change could also be deemed as different. This could cover a whole range of things including your first family holiday without your Ex/your child's mum or dad. These things can be very exciting too and embracing change can be a good thing, whilst modern society always 'advocates change' as a positive thing, not everyone may feel the same about change.

I am acutely aware of the impact of change and how it can sometimes make us feel a little wobbly, even if it is just initially. But if you were feeling wobbly, I'd like to think that you could steady yourself first before taking the next step.

10.2. Don't force it – how would you like it?

You have now found a new partner and I totally get that you are eager to spend as much time together as possible. It may well be that your living arrangements allow you to create this space. This could be when your child is with their other parent, or your work enables you to create these pockets of time.

Either way, these occasions could very soon become 'not enough', and you may start to feel cheated with not being able to spend time more freely with your new partner.

Firstly, I would like you to give yourself permission to enjoy the early stages of your new relationship, a bit longer. Enjoy the intimate time of the two of you together, where the day-to-day chores have not yet crept into your relationship. Relish each time you meet, as it still feels like a first date.

I am all too aware, that you might be itching for 'normality' or to spend time together cooking a meal or doing whatever it is that you are craving for. I would endorse by saying, 'slow down and enjoy'. This next part will happen soon enough, and when it does, the dimensions of the blended family will come with it.

In your previous relationship, you may have felt that your partner didn't get you. You may have been in an abusive relationship and never saw a way out, let alone a new mutually respectful one. Either way, you are hopefully now living your life – happy and content.

Stop, breathe and enjoy this time.

Let's take the example of parents sharing your child, one week on and one week off. When it is your 'week off', you may be able to enjoy just the two of you, you and your new partner. Doing things together, waking up together, snuggling up on the sofa and watching something on television you both enjoy.

However when changeover day arrives, you may not be feeling so content or happy. In fact, you may be feeling the complete opposite, and you may feel wretched at the thought of being apart. You may be trying to work out realistically when you can both next meet up. Even then being all too aware that the moments together will be hours rather than days.

I am fully aware that you may be feeling resentful with the week-on week off arrangement. This is natural and understandable but again; Do. Not. Rush. It.

At this point you may decide enough is enough and that you may feel your two families need to merge. This realistically will not mean fulltime, but enough to make 'changeover week' more fluid for you and your partner, including your child/childless weeks.

Like the train in the introduction, your child is playing catch-up. I strongly urge you to remember that all of you are unique. Yes, your youngest may have your temperament, your middle one may have your eye colour. Whatever traits they have, they are *them*.

Your new partner could be really into football for example, as is your youngest, and as their other parent had no interest, you may feel that's got to be a win–win right? No! Maybe over time yes and maybe never. Whilst that might be difficult to make sense of, try to.

The relationship with your Ex may have been fraught for you. This doesn't mean your child is looking to replace their other parent or indeed was ready for them to no longer be part of their daily living life. They may have been relieved when you finally separated but definitely have their own thoughts and feelings about a new partner being introduced into their lives.

Remember for them, they may well be introduced to two new partners! They may be introduced to one new partner, but their other parent is still reeling in the aftermath of the separation. This way, your child may be torn with seeing one parent's pain with the other parent's joy!

It's complicated, life's complicated, our bodies are complicated – like structures built with a highway of different interlinking parts – so why wouldn't a new partner being introduced to your family not be complicated?

Let me give you two examples to consider; firstly, a friend of yours may have introduced you to their new partner and you didn't take to them. The bonus here is, that you don't have to live with them.

The second example, could be when your child grows up and introduces you to *their* new partner and you feel they are not 'right' for them. When your child introduces their new partner to you, they may well have every finger and toe crossed. This is in the vain hope that you will approve of them and possibly even like them. (We are just talking dating here, not marriage.)

I can hear you shout at me, "But I'm just introducing them that is all," but it's not all is it? It's the first step of whatever might happen next. This could be their new step-parent forever or a new adult introduced to their life only to leave again.

So going back to the force it, let's change the word to *ease* it.

I remember working with a client once that so badly wanted both families to meet to allow them to spend more time together doing 'normal' things. The idea they came up with was definitely a forced situation for one of the children involved. When we were in session, we took the time to imagine how this may have felt if *they* were the one on the receiving end of the 'forced' blending. The client appreciated that for them, it felt both uncomfortable and that there was no escape and, they definitely wouldn't have liked it!

So we took a step back looked at what the 'urgency' was, and yes we came back to that good old word, *communication*. The client decided that they and their partner were going to explain the situation to their children respectively. They would ask them how best they could all go about working together to enable both families to spend more time together comfortably, easier rather than forced.

Reading this, it may seem obvious not to force the situation. You may even judge people in wanting to force the situation. Can I ask that you refrain from doing so. You are not them and they are not you. Instead ask yourself what *you* would like to do with your joining up of two families, and how you can communicate your needs and indeed listen to the needs of your child also.

Just like our body, which most of the time does what it needs to do without us consciously operating it, there are times when it needs our help. We listen to our bodies, let us listen to our families too.

I am not for one moment saying your needs are not important, they absolutely are. However I do think that it is important for each partner to speak to their children on a 1:1 basis to understand what it feels like for them. The partner could explain what 'bringing the families together' allows them to do, and this can only be a positive thing. Yep, we are back to the age-old C word, *communication*.

Use this opportunity to air everyone's fears, to 'release the power of the fears'. You may be incredibly surprised to learn what each person's fears are. Some of these you may never have even thought of.

Keep talking to each other. Talking opens up communication

lines and what that says is, 'I value you, I notice you and I accept you' – what a great lesson to teach your child and your partner too!

On the other hand, do not be surprised if your child wishes to meet your new partner and asks you to arrange this. As this is indeed what happened to me! At first, I felt flummoxed and was not prepared as I had no idea that my partner's child wanted this. I was also acutely aware that I hadn't thought this far ahead as I indeed was enjoying just 'our time' together.

My first reaction was to say I was busy, but how might the young person receive that? So, I told myself that I am the adult and it clearly is important for the child to meet me and so that's what we will do. Yes, I was nervous, that was totally understandable.

I know earlier in this section I talk about not forcing it, but that is coming from an adult. We must acknowledge and recognise that children have their own way of managing information and so if they ask something I.e. can I meet your new partner, be curious with them, ask what it would mean for them.

And like I also said, if they don't ask, then you will just have to have some patience.

10.3. Making time for yourselves and your new partner

I appreciate I have touched on a lot about *good communication* in the previous chapter. I do feel, that this is an absolute necessity when you want to spend time with your new partner. Also, if you start off communicating well, this will hopefully form the basis of communication in your relationship forever more.

The reason I say new partner, is because you may want to walk the dog with your new partner, or pop to the shops or garden centre with your new partner. This all might seem straightforward.

Rewind to before your new partner was in your life.

Previously, you used to ask your child to walk the dog with you or go to the shops. You may even have made strolling around the garden centre together, a 'fun' thing.

Can you see the change here?

Understandably your child may become anxious about this change, they may ask to come with you, or ask how long you are going to be. Remember they are getting used to you not 'needing' them. Up until now they were your go-to, they were the one you wanted to do things with, even if they didn't really want to do it at the time.

Their anxiety or want to know how long you're going to be will come from a fear of abandonment. The separation between their parents may have already come as a surprise, and they are either getting used to how it is now or are indeed getting used to the new family set up. And indeed they may now feel that they have been 'replaced'.

When there are any changes your child may feel nervous and seek reassurance. (Although their behaviour, actions and words may not appear to convey that!)

Rather than shrug it off or dismiss it, make some time and ask them about their friends, ask them why they spend time with their friends? This is now your opportunity to explain how you and your new partner are exactly that – friends too.

I would now like you to ask your child how they might feel, if you joined them say at the cinema or going clothes shopping with them and their friends? Admittedly they may say that they don't mind which is great, but ask them if they would like to you to join them every time. I'm fairly sure the answer would be no.

Having this conversation will enable them to understand that actually, what you have with your new partner *is* a friendship. Like all friendships sometimes you may just want one on one time and at other times, you are happy to have others involved.

Like I said at the start of this chapter, it is all about communication.

Make time to understand how your child may feel about not

being asked to go for a dog walk or stroll around the garden centre. Your child may also enjoy spending time with you and your new partner, which is great and this could be strongly encouraged – but why not agree an arrangement that suits all of you?

For instance, let's say you and your partner go for a dog walk and on your return all of you go and get an ice cream together. Another option could be that you and your partner go to the garden centre together and that evening you all watch a film together.

Just like a date night jar, you can have a family jar too where everyone puts ideas in (they don't all need to be costly). It could be that at the weekend you all go for a dog walk together for example.

The thing to remember here is that the difference between your current relationship and the one with your child's biological parent, is that your child probably wasn't around in your courting days.

It is really important to be aware that you may feel irritated that your time with your new partner seems to be encroached upon by yours or their children. That's not the children's fault, I understand no one asked for this, but more than likely they definitely didn't.

I appreciate it may feel like a bit of an effort and you might be asking yourself, 'Why does everything feel so difficult?', when all you want to do is go for a walk with your new partner. Depending on the age of your child, you may be going through the same thing too one day or have already gone through it, when your child no longer wants you to take them shopping or hang out with you.

Can you remember, or imagine how that feels? You may have felt rejected or unwanted, felt they were ungrateful after everything you have done for them. Again, this is how *you* were feeling not them, but nonetheless it is important for you to acknowledge the impact that it had on you, even if it was for that brief moment in time, when you suddenly felt 'uncool'.

If your child's other parent is estranged or lives further away, they may see you as their only parent and don't want to 'lose' you to your new partner. They don't want to feel forgotten and abandoned.

Please do not feel that this section is about making you feel bad for wanting to spend time with your new partner that is not what this is about at all. But depending on the length of time there has been between the separation of their parents and the arrival of the new partner, for a long time it may have been just you and your child.

You may recall my mum saying to my sister, "Well at least I have you." Well I do wonder how my sister felt, when a new man appeared in my mum's life? Did it feel too late to now ask to live with our dad, had that boat sailed?

This is not about guilt-tripping, this is about consideration and introducing your new partner into your child's life and about creating an enjoyable time for you and your partner.

Another important part to this is explaining to your partner how you feel when you are unable to see them on a 'child week'. Look at ways on how you can work together to reassure one another.

I cannot stress *honesty* enough at this time! If your new partner is asking you to phone them or pop round and it is not going to be possible, or it could be too stressful for you, say "As much as I would love to see you or speak with you, I won't be able to on this occasion" – that's perfectly ok.

This is your new relationship, so rather than create the same dialogue and 'contracts' that you had with your previous partner, now is the time to create new 'contracts/dialogues', ones that will work for *all* of you.

All the time you are developing this relationship, check in with yourself that you are happy with how things are going, that you feel your relationship is mutually respectful and considerate. Your aim is to work towards an interdependent relationship, whereby you can both work together but also independently. This way you both flourish as individuals and as a couple.

Too often people can 'lose' themselves in relationships or

put their needs to one side (as it may be deemed as selfish not to). This is not selfish at all, it is called 'self-care'. What can happen, is in the present you may not mind having your needs met, but be aware as this can create resentment over time.

So to recap, enjoy your time doing things you both like and allow yourselves to learn new things – together and individually.

10.4. Sleepovers help!

Never underestimate the power of a sleepover – they can contribute to a more harmonious home more than you may imagine, here's how:

As a young person, I simply loved sleepovers and over the summer holidays my best friend and I practically lived with each other the whole time between our two homes!

Now I'm not saying that's the way to go (although I am grateful that our parents allowed it), but a sleepover can help in many different ways. Admittedly as a stepparent, I was never too keen on having another child stay over, we already had three that I found at times challenging, but here is how the sleepovers worked:

Having a sleepover at your own house enables your child, be it biological or stepchild, to have a distraction for themselves. They entertain themselves and actually give you and your partner some breathing space. Suddenly you don't need to be the one to find something for them to do or indeed what may feel like, them listening in on every conversation that you are trying to have.

A sleepover provides your child with some much-needed young persons' time. A time for them to talk about their stuff and interests etc. It frees them up to be young again and perhaps for that moment in time, not to feel vulnerable or that they are being 'pushed out'.

I appreciate you are not intentionally pushing your child away, but if you're not actually naming it, your tone or actions will be saying, please can we have some adult time – i.e., time without you. A sleepover provides this opportunity and everyone benefits, so it is definitely a win–win.

Sleepovers are generally reciprocated, so your child gets to stay at a friend's house, this not only gives you some potential adult time, it again gives your child autonomous /independent time too.

The other benefit is that when there is more than one sibling in the house, or a blend of children from both parties, when a child is absent for the day/night, the dynamics in the house can change quite dramatically.

The way our household dynamics worked: my eldest stepchild lived with us full time and I mean full time. In the end it probably equated to two days a year that they would see their other parent and as much as I understood why, I never pushed or encouraged them to go, as I trusted their thoughts and feelings. Even though, I was acutely aware that this meant my partner and I rarely had the house to ourselves.

So, as you can see, I have lived through a variety of challenges being part of a blended family. Thankfully we have all come out the other side, one way or another.

Let us go back to the middle sibling. When the other siblings were enjoying sleepovers, it provided space to manoeuvre more freely, in as much as they didn't feel the need to be the 'third' parent to their younger sibling. They also didn't have to witness the relationship between the younger sibling and myself, which caused them great distress. So for them, they also got to have time out.

For our eldest, when either our middle child or youngest had a sleepover they relaxed more, because my other two stepchildren almost seem to come as a pair. The pattern was, that they would start winding each other up and then, jointly started winding the older sibling up. The house could in those days slump into battle stations in less than five minutes after they arrived 'on our week'.

So as much as some weeks there could be six of us (with the additional child), it was ok. Even if a sleepover wasn't happening, but a friend came over, again, this was encouraged.

I feel it is so important for young people to be exactly that, *young*. Let them play, let them be free of any family troubles or concerns even if it is for a few hours only.

I would say though, if your child is having a lot of sleepovers at other people's houses and they are not inviting their friends back, then raise this tentatively with them. Ask what it is about their friends' home that they like. Get them to describe their friend's home, what pets they have, who lives there. What sort of things do they do when they stay over.

You may be surprised by how your child describes it – or indeed what the attraction is.

My best friend's house was so relaxed. We were able to literally turn their bedroom upside down and dismantle the beds in order to make a camp. Tea was on tap, with their mum knocking on the door with what seemed like every five minutes offering us a cup. On school holidays, we would stay in our pyjamas most of the day, there were no chores, no demands, only to stay safe and look out for each other – it was incredibly easy and carefree.

Their parents were incredibly hardworking people who both worked full-time and sometimes had a second job too. However when they were home, they always managed to create an atmosphere of me feeling being both heard and noticed. We were always considered. If Enid Blyton had written about summer holidays and staying over at a best friend's house that would have been *the* house!

Importantly this became my safe haven when my parents split up. Nothing had changed in my best friend's home, everything was still the same safe environment, which I had been used to for the last six years – this proved invaluable for me.

My best friend's house gave me the opportunity to relax and be me – with no extra stresses and no high expectations. We tended to eat our dinner in my friend's bedroom, or one of their siblings' bedrooms, depending on who we were hanging out with at the time – it was good – it was much needed respite at a very difficult, painful and upsetting time.

Think about when you had a sleepover, how it was for you and if you weren't able to have sleepovers, how was that also?

All I ask, is that you give it a go for your child to try for at least a few times, just to see the impact it can have, you never know, you may be pleasantly surprised.

11. A New Family

Before I start about a 'new family', I looked up families and the internet told me about a variety of different named families. One in particular that stood out for me was the 'nuclear' family, which appears to be portrayed as an 'original/core' family i.e. both parents and children of the same family, that in the eyes of the media are seen as 'a happy family living in total harmony'.

Well, whilst I'm not saying a family living in total harmony doesn't exist, although I do think it might be in the minority. My point is, that my book refers mainly to the 'new family', and not what can be referred to as the 'nuclear' family.

Also, a 'new family' may be when a couple has a child and their unit changes from a couple to a family. In this chapter though, we are looking at what happens when a blended family comes together, and how that 'new family' may or may not look. Indeed, just like each person's *Facebook* page is unique, so is your own blended family.

So, just like the ripples in the pond, you have looked at your new relationship in the previous chapter, and so this is about the further ripples/dimensions of your 'new family'.

Just like the 'allotment' in a previous chapter, before embarking on your new family allow yourself and your partner time to consider these various chapters, or concerns you may have, about how things may or indeed may not work. When you give yourself the time to look at potential outcomes both positively and negatively, this will hopefully provide you with a more realistic understanding.

I do not expect you to be experts in this area before introducing your partner in to your new family. You probably weren't an expert either, when you got married or began living with your previous partner, or when you had your first child. I am fairly sure though, when you were having your first child that you may have done some research, read some books or you spoke to friends. So why would you not give yourself, your revised family and your new partner the best starting point possible, that's all I am saying.

Speaking to friends that are already part of blended families may be a good place to start, asking them what worked for them, what they may have changed if they could. Ask the adults, not their children, how the children reacted.

I appreciate your child are not theirs, but you may pick up some tips. It also might be worthwhile (as per chapter 2.1), letting the school know of these recent changes. In doing this, you are putting up potential support pockets for your child. Therefore should they find it hard and are unable to communicate how they are doing, other people may be able to pick up their 'unfamiliar' signals.

11.1. How many 'parents' grandparents etc.?

This chapter feels a bit like who's who? There are all different names for family members, mum, dad, brother, sister, aunt, uncle, nan and granddad to name a few.

What happens when the blended family comes together? What happens when there is a mum and a mum, will one of the mums be called mumma, or mummy Jane to differentiate between the two? Again, allow yourself some time to process what it might feel like having your name altered.

There are lots of different angles to the family, but to start with, let's look at it like a pebble hitting a pond and the ripples going outwards. Let us literally peel back the layers to the core of each family. Just to clarify, when I refer to family, I am referring to each party coming into the family e.g.

The 'nuclear' family previously:

a) mum, dad, brother, sister, or mum, mumma, brother, sister

The separated family, now has two parts:
b) mum, brother, sister
c) dad or mumma

Your new partner's family:
d) Fred
e) Sonia and her son Paul

Even though Fred is entering into a relationship with mum, he will be classed as his own family. I apologise if I have lost you now, but keep reading and hopefully we will get there together.

Ok, so the core of the family in b) has three members. Each member separately has their own view (which could change) on what they want to call 'new' family members. They might want to call Fred 'dad' or 'pa' for instance, or Fred. One child might want to call Fred 'dad', and the other call him Fred.

I appreciate you may have assumed they will call him Fred – never assume. Again, this could be a conversation for you and Fred to have prior to introducing them. Fred may not ever want to be called dad or pa.

I was at wedding recently of a blended family. The morning after the wedding as we were leaving the hotel, the child of the other parent called the bride mum. The brides response immediately was, 'Oh no, we won't be using that word!' Wow, as an adult I was dumbfounded and felt a blow to the stomach, I have no idea how the young person received it!

It is absolutely the bride's prerogative to not want to be called mum, however I wonder was that ever discussed before the wedding and indeed conveyed to the young person? I'm presuming, that it may not have been given a moment's thought as they didn't *expect* that to happen. See how it can be a good thing to explore the 'unexpected'.

At this point it is important to acknowledge that there is no right or wrong. However, what is important is that each person is heard and the other members of the family can share how they feel about that. As a mum, you may feel opposed to Fred being called dad, confused even why your child may want to do that. It may be, that already in the back of your mind that you hope they will call your new partner dad in the future. (Remember – that's your thoughts, not your child's.)

If you notice, we haven't even brought the biological dad into the discussion. He will probably have his own view, as to who will be called what. The point of all of this though, isn't about getting lost in the 'What's right and what's wrong', but noticing how each 'core' family member feels.

Then allow each person's thoughts to be considered – slowly. Ideally together as the 'core' family, you are able to work out the names for new family members. Again, remember the 'names' may change as members of the family could become closer. For example, Fred becomes dad over time. This will empower the children, in particular bearing in mind their world has been ruptured previously without them having a say.

I remember my sister and I referring to my mum's new partner as Slimy Mike, obviously not to his face, as we were brought up to be polite and respect elders. So, we were respectful to his face, but were we ever asked how we felt, the answer was no! Or for that matter, did our mum ever question our name for slimy Mike, again the answer was no.

A friend of mine referred to their dad's wife as Lilo Lil – this was between them and their sister. It united them when they were young and going through the separation of the family and it continues to unite them today. And as for my dad's second wife, that's exactly what she was referred to 'his wife' and nothing else. She meant absolutely nothing to me and was not even worthy of having the title stepmum!

So hopefully that gives you a little insight of the importance of talking this through and not just assuming that Fred's parents will automatically become your 'core' child's grandparents for example.

Again, thinking back to the 'train station' (pg 12) you may have already covered lots of subjects including family members with your new partner. You may have even met some of them. Remember your child will most of the time be playing catch-up. It's a bit like a surprise, where we sometimes have to ask ourselves, who is enjoying the surprise more, the person giving or receiving?

When I work with my clients and indeed talk with my own friends about their family members, there is such a huge expectation that because they are *family* we 'should' like them (see 15.1). But actually no, it isn't a given and once clients and friends have allowed themselves to take the pressure off 'liking' a family member, it feels so much easier.

I worked with one client who felt that their stepparent's Ex really got them and understood them. Being understood felt they were heard, considered and accepted. My client felt a sense of great conflict, betrayal almost, between their biological parent and their stepparent's Ex.

They eventually learnt to acknowledge and accept that their biological parent couldn't provide this space for them and yet an adult who wasn't part of their family could. As we explored this together, they relaxed and allowed themselves to enjoy what was their 'unconventional' relationship.

Your new revised family is possibly getting used to a new adult and or siblings in their life, and adding further to the potential anxiety, it may also be that you have moved into your new partner's home as a family.

If a change of home is the case, again, endeavour to have adult conversations between adults and not with your child no matter what age, about the impact of whose home is whose.

Another client of mine had two homes, one with their mum and stepparent and one with their dad and stepparent. The house where their biological dad lived, was originally the stepparent's home.

There were many times when the stepparent commented, "I never get the place to myself anymore" or their actions were consistently moving the young person's belongings to 'their' room. This made the young person feel like 'they were being 'erased' from living there.

Remember this is how the young person felt, but coupled with the comment on never getting the place to themselves it can definitely magnify the sense of not being wanted.

I am aware that I have said this more than once, but if you notice your partner saying anything like this or acting in certain ways, which could be *interpreted* (keyword here) as not wanting the child, you should speak to your partner – yes you may find it uncomfortable – but the ramifications of their actions is not healthy.

As an adult I have been in a relationship where my personal artefacts were always tidied away and to me it felt as if, there was to be no trace of me in my partner's home. As an adult I can tell you I both felt confused and in conflict, as to whether this person wanted me in their life or not – imagine how that may feel for a young person.

I ended up sharing how it made me feel with my new partner. They acknowledged, that they were doing it and took on board how it made me feel – furthermore, they reassured me that it certainly wasn't because they wanted to 'erase' me.

11.2. You're not my mum!

Well maybe it was only my fear when I became a step-parent, but I was aware that I dreaded the day that those words could be used towards me. Thankfully I have to say they never have been uttered and indeed having had step-parents myself, I may have thought 'You're not my dad' in my head when my parents partner may have said something, but I too have never uttered those words.

I am however very aware that "You're not my…" has been received by many a step-parent.

The one thing that I will touch on when a child says the above words or something similar, is even though you may feel rage, sadness, or despair for example, we need to understand what does it mean for the child to say that? What exactly are they saying or indeed not saying that has provoked them to make that statement?

Admittedly if they have just said those words, it realistically isn't the right time to explore what is going on for them. I recommend for you both to take some time out and either yourself or your partner could have a chat with your child to find out what provoked them to say that.

It may be helpful to know that even though it will feel very personal because yes, it was directed at you but, it more than likely is something that is going on for them that they are not happy with – please try to bear that in mind. I appreciate that could be easier said than done.

This section, is about recognising the impact of how your child may feel (the key word here is may) about your new partner, your new partners child or your partners wider family.

Your child could be comparing your new partner to their other parent which is natural and it is paramount to give your child the space to get used to this new adult in their life.

Relationships take time and you need to give your child the time to settle in with this new person in their life. Your new partner may have a child also which your child will also be thinking about too. They may be thinking about how they feel if this other child is spending more time with you, or if this step-child comes to live with you full-time and yet your other child is week on / week off that could also stir some thoughts and emotions.

As I continue to hopefully reiterate throughout this book, is that there are no right or wrongs, but giving your child the space to share their worries, concerns and thoughts / observations are a great way to start.

I totally appreciate that what your child may say, could bring up emotions or reactions for you too of course and that would be completely natural. However allow your emotions to settle and then talk and keep talking. Just because your child hasn't mentioned something for a while, do check-in with them and see how they are now feeling.

Yes, you may not want to stir a potential 'hornets' nest' however, if the hornets' nest is there it will stir up at some point whether now, later or much later for your child and even into their adulthood.

12. You're getting married

So you are getting married! Congratulations! Whoop Whoop!

And yes, I do genuinely mean that. When my partner proposed to me, I was ecstatic and over the moon. I was acutely aware that I wanted to savour their proposal, just the two of us, before hearing how the children would respond…

I am really pleased for you – Brownie's honour. You and your partner are hopefully in a really good place, and your blended family is more than surviving the various nuances, that only a blended family can bring!

However, as excited as you are about your big day, before you run off and start planning everything, take some time to look at any potential impacts on the other members of your new (or maybe not so new) family? Again, here I am only referring to your immediate family – parents/stepparents and children.

I expect thinking about your Ex is not one of the things on your to-do list, however it is important to include this with regards to impact. If your child is in contact with them, then this subject will come up and this should *not* be down to your child to tell them. You may have crossed your arms now and be frowning at me – how dare I bring up your Ex, you're getting married and they have no right/need to know about it!

Ok, calm down, let's look at this logically.

You may want your child to be at your wedding, when it's their other parent's weekend to have them. In this instance, cooperation could help.

After you are married, your child may soon have a 'different' surname to the rest of the family members in their home, where they spend most of their time. Speaking to your Ex about this and asking them to reassure your child that even though they are not often (in the Ex's home) they are still part of the family. This could help to comfort the child.

I am not here to cast a dark shadow over your happy news, all I am asking is for you to be tentative about the effect that this will have on your family and how to bear certain parts in mind when discussing this, as this important chapter understandably isn't just about you – apologies if you thought it was.

If you are still reading, well done. I wouldn't blame you if you cursed me and my book, tossed it into the bin or deleted it off your electronic device. I get it – your wedding day is 'kind of' all about you!

But do you know what, it still can be and realistically it will be – but with a little consideration for others (or a bit more than a little) your day could run more smoothly and emotionally easier for your loved ones and you to enjoy – that's all I'm saying.

You can do this, you've got this far, why would you want to throw away all your hard work?

12.1. What's in a name?

Our name is such a fundamental part of who we are, however I feel it can be taken for granted or not given much thought. I wonder how many times today, there has been a reference to your name, your *individual* name.

It's the middle of the afternoon as I type this, and so far today, I have changed address over the phone where I had to give my name. I received a parcel at the door and even though I didn't need to sign for it, I was already thinking that I will need to sign for it with my name. Also, I received post through the door with my name on it. I cancelled an online subscription and sent an invoice, both of which required my name.

So, what am I getting at you are asking? Well, through our names we know who we are. Yes, with titles that may define us more, or show how we wish to identify who we are, but our first name and more to the point our surname can act like an anchor. They give us the base to know where we came from.

As a person getting divorced, you might potentially not be able to wait to change your name back to your maiden name or something entirely different. Seeing your post arrive or doing any of the things that I mentioned above, with your Ex's surname, may trigger a variety of emotions when you see your surname, sadness, anger, disappointment to name a few. You may feel that, you have been 'anchored' or tied down to that name for way too long.

On the other hand, it might be that your current surname doesn't cause you any concern whatsoever. You and your current partner have decided to join together in a legal partnership, and you automatically accept or have discussed in detail, that you will be taking their name.

Now this is the part that can get a bit complex. This is where it could be really helpful before you share your news, be it changing your name by deed poll or through marriage of some kind, to consider your child in your new family.

I have previously referred to the ripple effect, try and do the same with the name change. You may find it helpful to grab a pen and piece of paper and write down, who may be affected by the name change and what the impact could be on them. We say may, because however close we are to someone we don't actually know them and their thoughts. We may have an idea but we don't actually know.

I remember when a friend of mine was getting married and their young child took them to one side and said, "When you marry I will be the odd one out in the family, because you will all have the same name and I won't." Wow, I can't remember their exact age, but I think it may have been five years old.

The anchor for this child being the name that showed who they were and the core family they belonged to was changing, and for them it was a distressing thought.

An important part also to notice, is that for this young person they spent the majority of their time in the home, where they were going to be 'the odd one out'. So consciously or subconsciously they will be reminded throughout the day, that their name is different.

The ripple effect will continue into school too, as the children collectively may have a school family photo, or children might ask them why their name is different.

I am not saying for one moment that it isn't appropriate for you to change your name, but instead to consider the impact of doing so. Again, communicate to those involved using the inner ripples first and then moving to the outer ones.

On the other hand, another young person I know couldn't wait to change their name to their new stepparent's surname. For reasons unknown to me, the school seemed to take a long time in finalising this and the anguish it caused the young person whilst at school was incredibly apparent.

Each class, the young person waited for the register not knowing which name they were going to be called by. All the while wanting to change their anchor, which meant so much to them and yet appeared to not be of a high priority in the school. It baffled and frustrated me that one lesson knew their new surname and the next one didn't!

Again, children can be cruel and if some schoolchildren are given the opportunity to show someone who is 'different', there will be ones that will grab that and use it against them, as they did with the young person above. The child was tormented about what their 'real' name was.

Anyhow, I'll step off of my soap box, but hopefully this chapter will have given you time to consider your name and your children's name and any changes that may or may not happen in the future. You may have no intention of changing your name even if you were to marry your partner, however whilst you may not, remember your child may want to. Again, have this conversation with your children.

Ask yourself, if there is the possibility of your child having a double-barrelled surname? It may be prudent to speak to your Ex first (before potentially getting your child's hopes up) and indeed your child will probably have their own view on what name they may want.

It is always good to provide reassurance. People don't generally enjoy feeling vulnerable, so if that can be eased – great!

Your child may not even consider the name change as a big thing to them, but instead they may race on to what will happen on you wedding day. Children will obviously react differently, because they are their own unique person. So, if a child asks about one thing i.e., your potential new name or the wedding day, share the information with all the children, give them all the same information. Not necessarily together and even though they may not respond in a way that suggests they are concerned, give them the time and space to process what you have just told them.

Moving onto the day, think about how they may involve themselves or not in the wedding, again share your thoughts and ask them. Can I ask at this point to not put any expectations on them, or to be made aware of any expectations *you* may have.

Some things might not be on your radar, but where possible, speak to the wedding party to ask them to consider *all* of the children throughout the day. Sometimes the youngest child or the flower girl may receive more attention than the others for example. Whilst this may not happen intentionally, the other children may need 'looking out for' and therefore it is still a good opportunity to remind people of this role.

One may want to do a reading. Another may want to be an usher and another again may not want to be there at all – all of their choices are ok. With the one saying they don't want to attend, give them the option to change their mind, should they wish to do so. You may be relieved that they have said they do not want to attend – remember to not show or express your relief where they could witness it.

I never forget one wedding I went to where the groom started to talk about their children collectively. He then proceeded to talk in depth about his three and what sounded like an afterthought said, "…and then there's Kate's two" and that was all he said.

I have to say my heart went out to the bride's two children who had just heard their stepsiblings praised and congratulated and yet there was absolutely no recognition for them – shocking! Ok, I accept that the bride can't read the speech, but surely someone could have and in this process brought some thoughtfulness into it?!

I'll leave that thought with you…

13. Celebration days

Yay celebration days!!

Days where *Clinton cards* et al. makes huge amounts of money – well that's pretty much what they are there for - sorry for the cynicism! Yet admittedly cards do feature heavily in my world – I could and do spend a fortune on cards, I can pretty much find any reason to buy a card apart from general Christmas cards, which I – Do. Not. Do!

So, what's the hang up about celebration days, you may ask?

Well, again, I think it could be helpful to run through your calendar and write down all the days you currently acknowledge – birthdays, Mother's Day, Father's Day, Christmas, Valentine's etc. and next to each day, write a brief summary or bullet points, as to what those days *used* to look like.

I say 'used to', because you are now in a new blended family, which is no longer the same as your family once was.

Now write down or highlight the celebratory events which can no longer happen or may have to be done differently. Just like in (5.1), where I talked about blue and pink jobs, different parents may have undertaken different roles, say in birthdays.

For example, my mum always used to bake us a birthday cake and coloured it in the wildest icing, which no one could possibly have replicated! I recently made my sister a birthday cake and she said "oh where's the wild coloured icing"! So I have made a note to try and replicate mums colourful creations for my sisters birthday next year.

Or let's look at Father's Day. Previously, you may have bought your husband a card and a present from yourself and a separate gift from your child. However now, you may feel resentful acknowledging them let alone buying anything for him. Therefore, your child could find themselves in the predicament that they feel unable to ask you to help them buy a gift for their dad, as they are all too aware that you are not keen on him anymore - (understatement of the year!)

So, with this in mind, you need to understand that celebration days need looking at too.

Maybe you were made a big fuss of by your partner on Valentine's Day, your wedding anniversary or your birthday but obviously they are no longer there. The ghost of that tradition will still 'hang in the air', so how can that be managed? And no, ignoring it isn't really an option – well it is, but one that I wouldn't accolade!

Your new partner or their family may have their own traditions at Christmas or New Year, so conversations around these could be really useful. If your Ex has a new partner themselves or not, they may want to carry on with *your* family's previous traditions. How might that be for you and your child?

Again, sorry to repeat myself, all I am hopefully doing is to encourage you to look at these important dates (even if they don't feel that important now). Also, after each date reflect upon what worked and what didn't work quite as well as you had hoped.

13.1. Oh dear it's Christmas

Christmas is an incredibly emotional time of year – another understatement of the year!

It appears to consume everyone and everything. Christmas seems to come with its own set of expectations, demands and costs, and that is without looking at the needs of your new blended family. Now, I am not saying that non-blended families have a super easy, picture perfect Christmas, I'm just saying a blended family has added dimensions.

I feel an important aspect to consider, before we delve into looking at the blended family Christmas time, is to look at our Christmases of the past and to be completely honest with ourselves.

Exercise time: I would like you to grab a pen and piece of paper, and just try this exercise with me;

First of all, I would like you to write down how you would like Christmas to be or imagine how Christmas could look if you had a magic wand. Take your time with this, be creative and most importantly have fun! (Ideally grab some coloured pens, so we can really get your creative juices flowing!)

Ok, whatever you have written is completely right, because they are your 'Christmas dreams' for want of a better expression.

Now, I would like you to divide this next part into two:

Part one is of Christmas in the past, i.e. when you were a young child and how Christmas was for you, good or bad. Part two, is of recent past Christmases, before you became a blended family.

It could be, that you have two Christmases in the recent past, one when you were with your 'core' family, partner and child, the 'nuclear' family i.e., both parents and children of the same family. The other when it was you with or without children.

With both Christmases, you may find that you are noticing all the positives or negatives, and what I would ideally like you to write down, is a *true* reflection of how it was, so both positives and negatives.

I appreciate this may be upsetting, but this is about us drawing out emotions of your past that lay dormant until Christmas rears its head again. Then what happens is that the plug is pulled and your dormant emotions spill out or rise to the surface, and therefore become the foundation to Christmas once again.

It is almost as if the play has already been written, and now all that is left is to assign the cast. Your previous script just needs dusting off and hey presto, Christmas of past clashes with Christmas of present – oh no it doesn't – oh yes it does!

The whole point of that exercise is not to make you feel sad, or 'What's the point, as Christmas is always a let down', or 'It won't ever be like it used to be'. Instead, what this will hopefully enable you to do is to appreciate that the past is the past, and you can now write a new script for Christmas, or come into Christmas without the expectations of times gone by.

Indeed, part one will hopefully have allowed yourself to notice what your dreams of Christmas are. With this new information, you can look at what may be achievable and what may not.

We all set ourselves a 'bar'. You may call it expectations or striving to better yourself, but generally the 'bars' we set for ourselves are much higher, than we would ever set for anyone else. The 'bar' we set for people that we care for is always achievable. I acknowledge that once they have achieved that bar, we may re-set it.

Now that you have your Christmas dreams written out, you can start to lower your 'Christmas bar' – (Christmas expectations).

It may be, that you have already experienced several Christmases as a blended family, and they haven't quite worked out how you would like them. If that is the case, I would recommend reading chapter (14.2).

The difference with blended families, is that some of the parts are out of your control, namely how the 'the Ex' does or doesn't do Christmas.

Depending on the age of your child, talk to them about Christmas, ask them how they feel about it. I understand it may be difficult to hear how they are feeling, and in some cases if a parent is estranged, you may not be able to make them feel better about it.

But what you are doing by having these conversations is saying it's ok that they feel that way. It's ok to talk to you about how sad or angry they are feeling, instead of feeling that they cannot say anything because they want to protect your feelings.

How you are feeling about their estranged parent also needs to be looked at. Ideally discussing this with a friend or family member and not your child, no matter how old they are. Your child may have fallen into the role of the absent father, but they may not necessarily want that role or responsibility. (See chapter 7.3)

One way to look at Christmas is to look at each year as a practise run. Each year, you can try out a different way of 'doing Christmas'. Reflect on what worked and what made you want to scream or indeed scream! Above all, do not brush it under the carpet hoping it to all to be forgotten, and that next year it will 'automatically come good'.

As I have repeatedly mentioned, *communicate*!

Communicate to your partner how you see Christmas playing out. What could be changed or adapted to make it less daunting or less full-on. However it feels to you is valid, because these are your feelings. Your partner may view it differently or be dismissive saying "It wasn't really that bad." That is their view, which equally needs to be considered.

The main thing is that you are both talking about it, and if it is deemed appropriate include your child. If you can, get everyone's expectations out on the table or on the *WhatsApp* group. This could be your starting point, and remember you are not expected to find an answer immediately.

You and your partner may decide to come up with an alternative Christmas, that's ok, then you can share this with your child. However, let me remind you that the 'ghosts of Christmas *shoulds*' will without a shadow of a doubt rear their ugly heads.

Again do some research, look at how other countries or friends celebrate Christmas or indeed not celebrate it. Instead of staying at home, you may decide to use the money and have a holiday instead and maybe that becomes your 'new Christmas tradition'. Do allow yourself time to play with ideas and do not give yourself a 'bar' whereby you have to 'get it right' first time.

You and your partner may wrestle with your decision, it is really important that as and when the past shows itself, talk about it between you. Explain how the 'shoulds' are making you feel and then go through your new Christmas plans, and how and why you came to making them – write this down, so that you can refer back to your notes at any time.

Now take a moment (or longer if possible) to imagine your new take on Christmas. As the saying goes, 'practise makes perfect', so keep practising this. The more you do it the more it starts to feel more comfortable and less of a conflict of the expectations of the past.

In order to create your Christmas, compromises may have to be made. Do not look at compromises as a negative, but as a component to reaching a deal or agreement where everyone benefits and actually enjoy what may have previously been a difficult time.

In fact, maybe the crucial wording here is 'managing expectations' in a new and different way.

13.2. Mother's/Father's Day

It's funny isn't it, in a world where the words diversity, ethnicity and culture are constantly mentioned on a daily basis and yet regarding Christmas, people presume that *everyone* celebrates it.

For me, this feels the same as Mother's Day and Father's Day.

My dad was massively anti-Father's Day (and Mother's Day). He felt it was completely commercial and in no uncertain terms did he want us, his children, to participate in it. Well for a child, let me tell you, that was tough and one that I often went against. Whilst there didn't appear to be peer pressure about celebrating these days, can you imagine the internal conflict of wanting to celebrate your parents and them telling you not to!

I find it interesting on reflection, my dad's view was overshadowed by the commercialism of it. How could I not buy him a card, what does that make me? Why can't I choose to celebrate him and show my love for him on Father's Day? Even if it is commercial!

Even though my dad had the same view about Mother's Day, I felt he could only voice his opinion about Father's Day. I felt he could not dictate how I chose to acknowledge Mother's

Day, and therefore I very happily celebrated Mother's Day!

I would go all out for my mum, as I totally appreciated everything she did for us, be it cooking, taxi-ing to and from friend's houses, creating a lovely home and looking after us – she deserved to be acknowledged!

So how does it work when you become a stepparent? Well like most things in a blended family, there are a multitude of dimensions, thoughts and feelings, and Mother's/Father's Day is no exception!

Let's break this down into sections:

As a stepparent, as you are possibly beginning to learn, there is no rulebook, there are no givens. This can be particularly tricky for children at school, when other parents, kids and teachers may assume someone is their mother or father. Or on a 'Parent's Day', they may make cards for parents during an art lesson.

Do teachers consider the impact this may have on children in blended families or who may have an 'absent' parent? What conversations take place with those children who are of blended families? What choices are they given as to what they want in their cards? Or indeed whether they want to make a card, or do a different task altogether.

Remember, children generally want to please adults, to be accepted and get recognition, so teachers need to adapt their terminology, when certain tasks refer to family, ethnicity and culture.

As a stepparent whilst *you* have been automatically given the title of stepparent, this doesn't mean that you will automatically be recognised on Mother's or Father's Day – as the old saying goes, never assume!

Now whilst you may feel and possibly are, carrying out motherly/fatherly duties, it is not a given, that this will be recognised by either your partner or your stepchild.

Similar to the Christmas exercise, take some time to see, how you feel about that day. Would you like to be recognised in the parental role that you feel you are doing? If so, talk to your partner about this. It may be that the two of you go out for a meal, or your partner may buy you flowers.

But, and it's a big BUT, it may not be appropriate to do this on the actual celebratory day. You could choose the date that you became a family living together, or you may choose to do it when your stepchild is at their other parents' house.

If the children ask about the flowers for instance, be honest and say they have been given to you, to thank you as recognition to your contribution to the family. It is important to consider your feelings, and your stepchild's feelings need to be considered also along with your own child's too.

The biological parent may need to have tentative conversations with their child to hear their views. Indeed, it may not take a genius to know that one of the children definitely does not want to partake in that day, as they have a mother already and you are certainly not another one.

Also, be aware of the different dimensions between siblings, between your biological and stepchild. Of how your biological child may feel about a stepchild giving you a card and seeming to 'claim' you as their mum. Another sibling may find this challenging and struggle with keeping their feelings in, as they may see this as being disloyal to their biological mother.

My recommendation is never buy a card/gift on behalf of your child for a stepparent. If they are young, you are setting up a 'should' for the future (see 15.1). This will not only become an expectation between the adults, but is likely to also make your child feel, that they have no say.

As a result of a card/gift being bought on their behalf, they are unable to say how they are feeling about the situation in order not to upset either the biological parent and/or the stepparent – and here becomes the unwritten contract, which maybe neither of you signed up for!

Again, communication is key. Communicate to your partner how you feel about the prospect of 'Parent's Day'. What your hopes are, or how you would like to celebrate/acknowledge your part in their child's upbringing. Ask your partner what used to happen, was it a big thing, or did it come and go and it was never acknowledged? If that is the case, that doesn't mean that your day can just come and go without being acknowledged. You may crave to have a card from your stepchild, but this is where your partner will need to mediate, not tell them, but ask the child how *they* feel about it.

If their child is of a certain age, they may want their other parent to help choose a card and gift for them. This may continue for several years until they are able to do so on their own. Again, if possible, this could be a conversation between yourself and your Ex – what are their and your views about 'Parent's Day'?

Whilst we are on the subject of your Ex, I accept *you* may not wish to buy them anything, but please do have a conversation with your child about Mother's / Father's Day. You are not telling them that they have to do anything, but you are giving them the option to do so, and that you will help even though you are no longer with that parent. Therefore please give your child the option to explore what they may like to do, as they could be too young to buy a card or present or not have the money to do so. Put your feelings about your Ex to one side and see what your child's needs are.

Your views could be very different, just like my dad's and mine!

Like lots of other holidays that have the commercial influence, 'Parent's Days' are no different. You simply cannot go anywhere or watch anything without realising that day is approaching.

So rather than ignore it, face it and talk about it. Check in with your partner how they are feeling about it, and just because you may have had the conversation once, you may need to have the conversation again and again. Just like those days repeat every year, different feelings can come up every year also.

I remember when my eldest stepson arrived at our home with a card and flowers for me, I was simply bowled over, because it was his choice (I hadn't had any cards from him all the years previously) and the words that he wrote were truly from him. After he left, I said to my husband, that I will never need another card again and I meant that. I felt I had been acknowledged in my contribution to his upbringing, and that was more than good enough for me.

14. As Time Goes By

Your blended family, may well be in the swing of things. You have all got into a new rhythm and life seems to have calmed down of sorts.

This chapter is really to keep you mindful, that even though life is ticking along – I am sure there are still the day-to-day challenges that life throws at you – and there can still be times, when you and your child may feel sad.

I would like to take this opportunity to reassure you that this is completely natural and to be expected. You have all have experienced a loss. You have experienced a loss of the family that was, the loss of a parent no longer living with them on a daily basis. This could include the absence of a parent no longer standing on the side of the football pitch cheering them on each Saturday and Sunday.

Yes, you and your child will most probably have got used to this new way of being, but there will be times when you and your child sometimes intentionally and sometimes not, will reflect on life before. It could be a song, a meal, a saying or smell like aftershave that triggers the past into the here and now.

This is no different to grieving someone who has died, yes it can get easier after the first year and first anniversaries, but it doesn't stop you from thinking about them on their birthdays or at Christmas, and this really is no different.

So, this chapter is about taking this into consideration, noticing changes in behaviour of your child and yourself. If you notice you are feeling a bit low, 'check in' with yourself, what's the date or time, has something happened that may have triggered your past?

Most importantly this isn't about being cross with yourself for 'allowing' it to happen. You are human, it's bound to happen. This is about going with it, not being too hard on yourself. Actually it is more about being kind to yourself and/or your child. Letting them know it's ok to reminisce and feel sad, that they can talk to you if they want to or not, or if they want to do something else, maybe watch a film.

Most of the areas, which we have covered in this book, can relate to our day-to-day general lives. The difference being, is when a rupture in your family happens, it hurts, it hurts A LOT. Yes, the wound will scab over, yes the scab will get picked and in time the scab will become a scar, but even in low temperatures the scar can still hurt, and so at times, you and your child can hurt too.

Be kind, be loving and allow you and your child to be accepting of these feelings – because they are yours and you all matter.

14.1. Sometimes I'm sad – weeks/months later it can still be hard.

Just because time has passed, this could be a year or two or more, family members may at times feel sad.

Sad with the loss of their previous family or the semantics of how the family 'used' to be. I remember reading in *Michelle Obama's* book where she explains how 'grief is so lonely' and I completely agree with Michelle.

I feel each person's grief, is as unique as their own fingerprint. So what one person may find difficult or sad could be the complete opposite for the other person. You and your child will both manage grief in your own way, there is no right or wrong here. However it is important to respect someone else's grief, even if it doesn't match how you feel yourself.

When you hear the word grief, you may struggle with the idea that that is how you are feeling, but grief isn't just attached to the death of someone or a furry member of the family. You may also not realise that you are grieving and that's fine too.

This is really about not being hard on yourself or your child, but instead just going with it, acknowledging how you feel, giving yourself some space to do what you need to do. When you are ready, after a while you can carry on just as you were.

I feel it is really important to recognise that there is a considerable amount of grief attached to a family separating. When I talk about families separating, the family doesn't have to be 'legally' attached to qualify, it could be a parent's girlfriend or boyfriend.

Remember the chapter about learning new family members names and the ripple effect of the stone hitting the pond, and considering each person's view? Well the impact of separating (again) will trigger the undoing of what was previously and a whole new array of losses, be it positive or negative – a loss is still a loss.

A positive aspect for you could be that it felt like your child always had an axe to grind with your now Ex-partner, and hence you may no longer feel 'piggy in the middle' or like you are treading on eggshells to keep peace in the house.

However for your child, if that partner that has now left was in the mix of their 'original/core' parents splitting up, 'what ifs' could come in to play for your child. They may start wondering, 'What if Fred hadn't met mum, could mum and dad still be together?'

If your child start showing signs of anger suddenly (this could appear out of nowhere), maybe the anger has always been there it's just now that it has been given an opportunity to vent.

Your child may also start to feel hope in their mind that you and their other parent may get back together, or again feel frustrated that now Fred has left the scene and their other parent has a partner, that there is a missed opportunity of you and their other parent rekindling.

Remember, even if your relationship with your child's other parent wasn't that great, in quite a few instances your child could prefer both parents to be together. If nothing else, life may have seemed easier for them. It is always helpful to bear this in mind, as I have said earlier on, children have great imaginations!

In chapter (10.1) I talked about my acer tree, even though the 'rupture' was about a year ago, or however long, it takes time to re-establish our roots (and perhaps they didn't want to re-establish their roots, as they were happy with where their roots were in the first place!). That was their home.

As a parent, or stepparent (even if that's not what you are referred to within the family unit), you will have your own feelings about, what is going on for you. During difficult times, you may think about throwing the towel in, or how your life used to be, or whether it would be easier being a single parent again.

Whatever your thoughts and feelings are, I hope you allow yourself to acknowledge how you are feeling. Explore what it is that feels like the missing part or what you may be missing out on. If you are comfortable enough talk this through with your partner or initially maybe a friend.

Give yourself the time to understand what it is that is going on for you – I can't stress enough how important it is to acknowledge your feelings, rather than dismissing them or shoving them to one side.

I appreciate you may not want those feelings or indeed feel like you are a bit silly or sensitive, BUT they are still very much your feelings. *You* count so it's ok to say to yourself, "Do you know what, I feel sad about X or disappointed with Y" – it is still ok.

Otherwise what tends to happen is like the child in one of the previous paragraphs, the shoved aside feelings will ferment and in time will find their way out in possibly not such a constructive way.

Experiencing these sad feelings may feel absurd, confusing or even get mixed up with doubt. Of course it's going to be confusing, if you were the one to end the relationship or frustrating because you thought you had 'got over them' and certainly don't want to waste any more feelings on them!

But you *are* experiencing those feelings, so maybe you could grab a pen and a piece of paper, write down how you are feeling and what you were doing just before you started feeling sad. This way you may work out what the trigger was, and then think about ways to help support yourself and write these down too. Then, when you have these feelings again you can refer back to these notes to help during this difficult time.

This can be helpful to do it with your child if they feel comfortable going through it with you. Again, what we are encouraging here, is that good old word *communication*. More than that you will be creating an accepting environment, where it is ok to talk about the past, as much as it is ok to feel sad at times.

If you notice your child's mood or behaviour changes for longer spells and in particular they are not keen to talk about it, then do speak to either your GP, or if their school has a counsellor or pastoral support person any of those could be good.

This no way reflects on you as not being able to do your job. Sometimes your child may prefer not to share how they are feeling for fear of upsetting your or worst still, feeling that they may cause disappointment in your eyes, which we definitely do not want them to be thinking.

Families are complicated. (Full stop.)

Whether they are nuclear, core, blended, separated, revised or however you refer to your family, you are not expected to have all the answers.

Be kind to yourself and reach out to your support groups as and when you need them.

14.2. The aftermath: what ghosts of Christmas past are you still carrying?

A good time to read or re-read this chapter is straight after or even during Christmas.

This will enable you to write down any feelings you have had over this period or what you felt went well, and what you might like to change for next year for example.

If you feel you may like to change things for the following year, I would strongly suggest looking at this sooner rather than later.

The thought of thinking about Christmas next year may feel too soon (it may be only a few days ago that you experienced Christmas). However, whilst it is still clear in everyone's mind it could be helpful to address the potential changes now.

As time goes by, people will tend to forget how they *really* felt about Christmas, and assure you and themselves closer to the time, that it was ok really.

If you were to decide to wait for the next Christmas season to happen, this could feel too late in people's minds to get their heads around changing. This may be because they will already be assuming that everything will still be the same, because why wouldn't it?

When I refer to the aftermath of Christmas, what I am referring to is 'core' family traditions. These could be summer holidays, or the way your 'core' family used to celebrate birthdays.

All families have characteristics; Dad arriving home on Christmas Eve marked the start of the Christmas break. As he no longer does that now and instead your child might be going to his on Boxing Day or possibly not at all. Your child's mum's new partner is vegetarian so Sunday Lunch has altered for example.

It isn't necessarily what you may assume as 'the big things' that can cause a family member to be sad. Like grief, the 'firsts' are tricky and difficult, i.e. the first Christmas, the first birthday, and the first Mother's Day.

Again what is important is communication. The *WhatsApp* group might have been long deleted, no problem, start it up again. Either reach out (if you're the one feeling sad) or reach in to the one who may have withdrawn or is showing signs of sadness.

I will use Christmas as an example seeing as it is pretty difficult if not nigh on impossible to ignore or not be part of.

By now, you may well have experienced several Christmases in your 'new' family. Each year as your child gets older, they may start to have their own idea of what they may like Christmas to look like.

So rather than take it for granted what has been done in the past, how would it feel to have an open forum of ideas about how Christmas could be going forward? I am not saying a trip to Lapland or sunnier climes, but possibly just a tweak could be considered. Or who is spending time with whom, or indeed what time or day changeover is between the two homes.

Like many day-to-day activities, we can fall into a rut or a groove might feel a little easier to accept. Either way we can end up doing things 'like we have always done'.

As an adult it may have fallen that on Boxing Day everyone comes to your house, but actually as the years have gone by, maybe you would like a Boxing Day break even just for once, or you may have become to resent it altogether.

Let me reassure you firstly, that none of these feelings are wrong or bad, you are entitled to them. What is important, is that you firstly acknowledge how you are feeling and then 'play' with the idea of what Boxing Day could look like if it was to be changed up, even just a little bit.

Like I said, the key to this is communication. How about, whilst you are playing with the idea of changing up Boxing Day, why not speak to your friends about what they do. You could ask them what they would prefer not to do or would like to do differently, and what they would like to keep the same. Explore your views with them, remember whatever their response is, it doesn't make your views wrong or that they need to be dismissed.

People can be really funny buggers, when it comes to Christmas. The 'shoulds', are so ingrained that people may not even realise they are obliging to them (see chapter 15.1).

Along with the media and American films, emotions, expectations and shoulds, I feel, become pretty much greater than at any other time of the year.

You may find it helpful to bear this in mind; good actors and good scripts create wonderful family films and commercials showing goodwill to literally everyone. This in turn can make the majority of people to strive to have the 'perfect Christmas'. (Even though, it is completely fictional.)

By no means am I pushing my opinions onto you, I would just like to give you the opportunity to look at Christmas from a different angle. Mary and Joseph weren't with family – just saying!

Once you have toyed with new ideas and now that you may have spoken to friends, now is the time to start communicating these ideas with your immediate family. Like the pond affect, start with your immediate 'core' family and work your way out to the other people, who will be affected by these changes.

First things first, speak to your family and explain why you are thinking this. Always come up with part-solutions rather than just saying, "I don't want Boxing Day to be like it normally is." It could be something really simple for instance a buffet for lunch, and maybe a *Waitrose* sandwich platter for tea, or even a take-out. Just something to give you a break?

Importantly again do not expect the family to be a) overjoyed with this new idea or b) have alternative solutions.

The reason behind this, is because; a) they have only just learnt about how you are feeling and the festive 'shoulds' will be high on the agenda and b) 'because that's what we've always done' (potentially said in a whining/screeching voice – or maybe that's my teenager side coming out?)

And c) give them space for them to 'play' with this new concept and to think up ideas rather than expect them to have them tripping off their tongue. Who knows what people might come up with, you may be pleasantly surprised? Just like the train in the introduction, they are playing catch-up.

Once you are all onboard, now is the time to start sharing the new adaptions of Boxing Day to the other people, who may also have previously been invited to your home.

When the revised Boxing Day has been agreed, or a few are still resisting, write it all down. Then agree to set reminders in your phones or devices, to remind everyone of the new agreement. This is also important, as believe it or not people will comfortably forget!

My birthday is in January, which is a rubbish time of year, people have no money, they are dieting and partied out and some are doing *Dry January*. The last thing on anyone's mind is eating and drinking a bit more!

So one year I declared to my family that we wouldn't be celebrating my birthday in January, instead we would do it in the summer. My family all thought it was a mad idea, but agreed to go along with it.

Well quellé surprise, when I announced we were going to celebrate my birthday in July, my family looked at me again like I was mad, and reminded me that my birthday was in January. They swore blind that we had celebrated it and that was that, absolutely no birthday for me that year!

So, remind, remind and *remind*. Ask your family to tell *you* how Boxing Day is going to be this year. This will confirm to you that people have taken notice and also have 'bought into' the changes. This may all seem like a faff and a lot of hard work. During those times of feeling like that, I would like you to imagine yourself on Boxing Day, with the adjustments that you have encouraged – now how does that feel? Chicken Korma anyone?

15. Never underestimate a 'bully' word

I hadn't really envisaged having this chapter in my book about the 'shoulds and the oughts'.

Yet as I was delving into the depths of where yours and your child's minds might wander, the shoulds kept popping up. The shoulds kept rearing their ugly 'bully' heads and I thought to myself, to enable you to have the 'courage to continue', then relieving yourself of the *shoulds* and the *oughts* could be a good starting point. (Even though it's towards the end of the book!)

There will be times, when you will be prone to being 'hard' on yourself. You will find yourself having turned into judge and jury, with very little opportunity for you to actually be 'nice' to yourself. You are probably unaware that you have become very skilled at writing yourself off or you doing yourself down.

As humans we have evolved, and we are now able to do the most amazing things compared to our cave man and woman days. However intricate our brains are, we still carry some strong traits dating back to those cave days.

I spoke in chapter (3) about, fight, flight and survival and this is in relation to that. Before I go further, I am not qualified in any way to say this as such, however this is my understanding and what I have experienced when working with many clients. (Ok, that's the disclaimer out of the way!)

Our brains are an amazing part of our body. However for simplicity reasons I am going to say our brain has a pair of weighing scales in it. On one scale it has a huge weight, like the size of a grapefruit and the other scale has one single pea.

I would like you to imagine that the grapefruit represents negativity and the pea represents positivity. As the grapefruit is more dominant, it can take a lot of work for positive thoughts (the pea), to override any negative thoughts (the grapefruit).

All is not lost though.

Over time through 'feeding' the pea and not the grapefruit, the pea becomes bigger. The pea will never dominate the grapefruit as our grapefruit (negative) part of our brain, is also our survival part so we do need it. But through not feeding the grapefruit it does reduce and in time so does the negativity.

With that all clear now and to help you doing this without any additional grapefruit supporters, I would absolutely encourage you to read (15.1). It takes time to get used to, it takes weeks to change a habit (apparently between 21 and 250 days), but I know for sure if you practice only this one, your life could become a lot, lot easier.

I expect you are thinking *really*? And I will respond by saying yes <u>really</u>!

15.1. The shoulds and the oughts

I feel the following point, is one of the most groundbreaking changes a person can make in my eyes.

Through my training and subsequent counselling career, if there was one thing and only thing that I could take away, this would be the law of the 'shoulds and the oughts'.

Why did it have such a significant effect you might ask? I will say, because it is so simple to understand, and so simple to grasp. Anyone can do it and *immediately* start feeling the benefit.

I love it when I hear friends and clients using the word could, it is so empowering and liberating!

Ok, so without further ado, let me share this with you…

We grow up programmed with the shoulds and the oughts, you ought to know better, you should know how to do that by now, etc., etc.

I feel that the word *should* is a 'bully' word in the dictionary. It bullies us into doing things on a daily basis, which we really might prefer not to do. Using the word *could* (instead of should) leaves us with a choice.

Let me give you an example; let's say you thought about going to the gym and your hearing yourself saying, "I *should* be going to the gym after work." As a matter of fact, you are finding yourself running late at work, you haven't stopped all day and you are feeling both tired and hungry.

However the 'should' will still be there, like a big pointy finger and you will feel bad. Even if you decide not to go, the 'I should have gone to the gym' will linger like a bad smell. It will definitely stay with you for the rest of the evening, and may also be there first thing in the morning after.

It could continue to 'hover' until you eventually go to the gym again. Even going to the gym may still not be good enough, as the *should* will be reminding you, that you didn't go the day before!

So how do we change that?

Ok, what you say to yourself is "I *could* go to the gym this evening after work."

You may decide to go, which is great, or you may decide not to go which is also great. The difference being is that there is no big pointy finger here, hence it will not linger with you for the rest of the evening – the 'bully should' is nowhere in sight, and therefore you won't feel bad about not going to the gym.

I expect you are saying to yourself, 'It can't be that easy' or you may doubt that it actually works.

The thing is, we are brought up being influenced by others, in their language, that we *should* do things instead of *could* do things. Think back to school when the teachers told us that we *should* know this or that, well actually, yes you *could* not *should*!

We can put ourselves and others under so much pressure, when we say should. Throughout this book there will have been times, when you undoubtedly have said the word 'should' either to yourself or out loud. (I tried my hardest to irradiate any shoulds so apologies if one or two slipped through.)

You may be telling yourself, that you *should* have behaved in a certain way, or your child *should* be getting on, with your new partner, or how Christmas *should* be for example. But all that is doing, is putting additional pressure and expectations on you and others.

Changing a should to a could takes time, it takes time for us to allow ourselves to not be hard on others and ourselves. You may already feel that the coulds are a get out clause – not at all. The coulds allow you the opportunities to do exactly the same things as the shoulds did. The difference being, is this is without the potential feeling of you letting yourself down.

Let me give you another example; imagine you have been invited out with friends. The reality is, you have had a really busy week, it's raining outside, you're tired and quite frankly you would like to stay in and do whatever makes *you* happy. Enter the 'bully should' telling you all the reasons, why you *should* go out with your friends.

So now let's change the should to a could. Indeed, you could of course go out with your friends, but *you* have recognised how tired *you* are or may not even be in the mood. As much as your friends may miss you not being there, I am fairly sure that they will understand, that you are actually really tired and will hopefully, want what is best for *you*!

Suddenly the word could may start to feel like your favourite jumper, onesie or even a hot water bottle on a cold winters evening – or whatever it is that makes you feel safe and ok in the world. The shift from using could instead of should allows you to think rationally about what is good for *you*, unlike the 'bully shoulds', who only think of themselves.

You will have probably had a lifetime of shoulds and oughts and changing that will take practise, but persevere and you will reap the benefits.

Let's break this down into further bite-size learning chunks;

First of all, start noticing when you say should or notice

when someone else says should, you may notice that you say certain shoulds all the time such as. 'I should be happy...' or 'I should do this...'.

Now, I would like you to rewrite your regular lists of shoulds to coulds. I could be happy... or I could do this... By changing *one* of your shoulds to a could, this will start to feel easier for you. Through emitting the shoulds, you will realise how hard you have been and generally are on yourself.

The shoulds will almost certainly be endless, I should make a healthy meal, I should be on time, I should be a certain size. These shoulds will be rolling around in your head – ALL THE TIME!

If you can practise, practise and *practise*, changing should to a could, I can assure you, that it will make a huge difference to your wellbeing. I have included this chapter in this book, because you are probably unaware how many times a day you are using the word should: how you should be a certain stepparent, how you should be with your Ex or how you should have been different then none of this would have happened.

I am not saying your shoulds are wrong, but when we change them to coulds, they *could* be more achievable. Or if you do not achieve them, you won't berate yourself for not doing something you *could* have done.

Life is hard enough!

Life is particularly hard with separation, divorce and stepfamilies.

So look at changing should to a could as a helping hand in a challenging world.

I'm not saying you should do it, but you *could* do it.

16. Counselling For Parents

It never ceases to amaze me how a parent can seem desperate for their child to have counselling.

Yet when I suggest to them, that they may benefit also, it is almost instantaneously dismissed – Or I receive the response, "I'm alright"!

I am wondering, if a counsellor was to suggest counselling for you, why not be curious about that comment and ask the counsellor what they feel, or what led the counsellor to make that comment?

When I have suggested counselling in the past to a parent, I possibly saw something that didn't seem to be sitting right with them. On the other hand, they may have described what was currently going on in their life and I definitely felt that they would benefit from counselling. Having that space to talk about whatever they want, uncensored, unjudged and confidential.

This is where I become curious, that you may shrug off what you are going through and yet not do so with your child? I wonder, have you even considered how you are 'managing' your current situation is potentially part of what is causing your child to behave in the way they are? This could be what has led you to getting *them* counselling in the first place?

Counselling still has a stigma attached to it, as you may feel shame or defeated at the thought of needing to talk to a stranger. Let me take this opportunity to share with you how some of my clients have felt; some have come because a loved one has encouraged them, some because they felt there were only few options left, or they had exhausted all the other avenues.

Some of my clients have not previously had a good experience of counselling, but have now decided to give it another go – and for anyone that has experienced that and carried on, I say a HUGE well done to them!

- Yes, making that first contact is tough.
- Yes, going to your first session can be painfully difficult (emotionally and physically – physically as much as you have to step through the door!).
- Yes, returning the next week is a bit of a challenge also.

As we unfold your situation during the sessions, counselling becomes more familiar and less shameful, embarrassing or whichever feelings you had before you started. You will start to feel heard, possibly for the first time in a long time, or indeed the first time ever.

You will also start to claim the space in the counselling room, claim yourself and dare I say it, start to enjoy this space. Each week you can talk about, whatever *you* want to talk about, and in whichever way you want to talk about it – simple.

When most of my clients are ready to 'fly the nest' after however many counselling sessions, they are genuinely pleased they did it and most often wish they had done it sooner – so what's stopping you?

16.1. How about you the parent having counselling? Now there's a thought

So, you have noticed that your child is potentially acting differently, it may be in their mood or behaviour, or they have become monosyllabic? (Please refrain from putting this into the 'that's teenagers/youngsters for you' bracket. It isn't helpful for you, and it certainly isn't helpful for them!)

At the end of the day you are their parent, and more than likely you will spot changes before anyone else. Alternatively it could be that the school has picked up on something.

Again, maybe your child's behaviour or manner has changed at school.

A friend or the mother of your child's friend may say something to you. Please do not take it as criticism, instead thank them for looking out for your child – it's a good thing (pea) not a negative (grapefruit) – (pg. 142).

When a child finds a situation difficult, painful or uncomfortable, whilst they may be able to speak to you about what is troubling them usually, if they are struggling then they will tend to act out their discomfort in different ways. For them verbalising what is going on could feel too much, or they may struggle to find the right words

One of the reasons your child may tend to keep quiet is to not upset you, not upset their parents. As I have mentioned previously, children are very quick to apportion blame to themselves for the reason that their parents are separating or divorcing.

Yes, you may say that is disbelieving, however that is how they may be feeling. Whilst I imagine they had nothing to do with it, I would ask that you acknowledge how they feel and reassure them, that it was not their fault.

As you are trying to understand why your child may not be able to talk to you, can I ask you to place yourself in your child's shoes, be it for the last hour, day(s), week(s) or even months. I would suggest starting with the last couple of days, then week.

As you try and rewind the recent past, notice what your child may have seen *(this is by no means bringing out the big pointy blame finger – let me make that perfectly clear)*. They may for example have witnessed you crying and I endorse that's a good thing. Too many parents feel their children shouldn't see them cry. In fact, what is that teaching them?? (Probably another should!)

Anyhow I digressed…

As you hypothetically wander around in your child's shoes, just observe what they may have seen or heard or indeed what they may have interpreted. Just like Chinese whispers, your child may have seen one thing and then finished the story off themselves. They may have overheard part of a conversation, be it on the phone or between their parents during 'changeover time', and again completed either the sentence or the reason for that conversation.

They may undoubtedly even have been able to turn it around in such a way, that the reason for their parents' cross words is because of them. Although this may of course couldn't be further from the truth, never the less this is how they interpreted the situation.

As you meander around, jot things down that you notice. At first you may not notice anything, because of the big pointy blame finger, but ignore this, as it is not helpful to you or your child!

If you have more than one child, take time to notice what each one may or may not have seen or heard. If only one child's behaviour has changed, look at the differences between your children. What friendship groups do they have, what hobbies or clubs do they attend?

By going through this, you may be able to see how one of your children has other ways to express their feelings, or be able to get out their frustration through football for instance.

You may be asking yourself, so what has this got to do with *you* coming to counselling?

Well your child will, whether you agree or not, could be protecting you. They will have seen and possibly still are witnessing the hurt and upset, which this has caused you. Therefore the last thing they will want to do is to cause you further hurt.

On the other hand, your behaviour may have changed and you may not be communicating as you used to do. Therefore the signals your child is receiving could be lay low, 'don't poke the bear' or in this case don't poke mum or dad!

What counselling will provide you with is a space, an uncensored space to openly talk about anything and everything that you want to. One of the many benefits of counselling is the uncensored part. This gives you an opportunity to unravel what is going on for you without having to consider anyone else's feelings other than your own.

When a counsellor says nonjudgemental, this means that, we want to hear it from your point of view. I say to my clients to imagine we are going for a walk, and I am half a shoulder behind you. This is just enough for me to see exactly your view and gain a greater sense of how it is for *you*.

You may have noticed when you have been speaking to friends, that you refrain from saying something or censoring certain details. This could be due to a myriad of reasons, including embarrassment, shame, judgement, or would rather they didn't know everything. It may be just in case you get back together with your Ex, or they are still friends with your Ex.

Censoring generally goes unnoticed, as you will tend to do it automatically depending on, who you are with. For example, when you are at work or with your own parent.

We all do it – it is completely natural. What the counselling space provides is that, over time, not censoring will feel more comfortable and even liberating for you.

Counselling also enables you to be *you*, not the parent, partner, Ex-partner or whatever other role(s) you have, just *you*! It isn't often, that you will have the time and space to consider you and your needs first and foremost.

You might be thinking 'Well that all sounds good on paper', but how does counselling actually work?

Ok, imagine a ball of wool with knots in it, some might be quite big, some small and some not obvious to the eye, nevertheless, they are all there jumbled together with everyday life. Sometimes the knots may trip you up or make you feel angry or sad.

Well together, we will look at the knots. We will work out and understand where they came from, and whether you still need them in your life. Slowly we will tease them out.

Some of the knots were never really yours, but you had them 'given' to you in life anyway. Eventually you will end up with a long piece of knotless wool and then you can roll it back up to whatever shape you want. (Not like a ball of wool in a shop, because that is not what real life is like.)

Once you start easing and freeing yourself of your knots, your child will notice a positive difference in you, and you will also notice how different you feel in yourself.

So when you say to yourself; 'What is the point of counselling, and will it actually benefit me?'

Instead; ask yourself: 'How *could* being 'FREE" of knots make me feel?

References

Collins., 2019
https://www.collinsdictionary.com/dictionary/english/rule
[Accessed 23 June 2019]

Kingsley, E.P. (1987) "Welcome to Holland" Available at
https://www.ambitiousaboutautism.org.uk/talk-to-
others/2015-04-09/welcome-to-holland-poemcoping-with-
diagnosis

Marked by Teachers:
http://www.markedbyteachers.com/as-and-a-level/psychology/
describe-five-different-types-of-families.html
[Accessed 9th December 2018]

Obama, Michelle (201X) 'Becoming' Penguin Books

Oxford Dictionary https://en.oxforddictionaries.com/
definition/hindsight
[Accessed 01 January 2019]

Phrasemix. (2019)
https://www.phrasemix.com/phrases/set-ones-expectations
[Accessed 23 June 2019]

Afterword

Thank you for reading, 'When Families End and Blend'. I hope that you may have been able to find some useful tools to help you navigate your way through separation, divorce and / or being part of a blended family.

This book isn't exhaustive in its content as you may well have come up with your own unique challenges.

Either way, I want to accolade you for acknowledging to yourself that you may be finding things difficult at the moment. If nothing else, I do hope this book reassures you that you are not on your own.

Welcome to our

family

www.ingramcontent.com/pod-product-compliance
Lightning Source LLC
Chambersburg PA
CBHW051725040426
42447CD00008D/985